More Praise for *The Power of Community*

"One thing business leaders don't need is another book filled with management theories that have never seen the light of day in the real world. *The Power of Community* doesn't have that problem. Howard Partridge offers practical wisdom built on decades of business experience. You can trust what he says."

    —Dave Ramsey, bestselling author and nationally
       syndicated radio show host

"I have seen it with my own eyes. People from all different backgrounds coming together for the purpose of learning how to make more money in the businesses that they own. Most come because they are stuck, frustrated, scared, and slaves to their business. Howard Partridge gives them the skills and knowledge they need to turn their businesses around. But skills and knowledge are not the game changer. *The Power of Community* is the game changer. People sharing the wins and losses, the tears and the triumphs, praying and crying together about everything great and difficult about business and life. At the end of the day we need to be surrounded by people who tell us that we have what it takes and that what we do matters. We have a choice. We can go through life doing the best we can with what we have. Or we can grow through life side by side with our family, friends, and team members. Yes, *The Power of Community* is a choice. Choose to read and apply this book and it will change your life."

    —Tom Ziglar, CEO, Ziglar, Inc.

"Today's most effective business leaders understand that when those they lead feel (and are!) truly valued, they are happier, more loyal, and more productive. And few things will inspire this more than the feeling of belonging to something special; in others words, an environment of community. In this book, the author, Howard Partridge, who has built a sustainably successful company based on these very principles, does an excellent job of teaching us how we can do the same."

—Bob Burg, coauthor of *The Go-Giver*

"*The Power of Community* is a masterful, comprehensive, and systematic resource for how to lead and craft authentic, prosperous, and dynamic communities both inside and outside your company! Howard Partridge's breadth of business acumen and thought leadership shine through in an engaging, thoughtful, and approachable set of ideas, tools, and principles for achieving interpersonal success and leadership significance! If you only have time to read one book this year—make it *The Power of Community*! Better yet, buy a copy for your entire team and your business colleagues so that together you can build communities of excellence that will sustain transformational success."

—Joseph Michelli, Ph.D., CCXP, New York Times #1 bestselling author of books such as *The Starbucks Experience*, *Driven to Delight*, *The Zappos Experience*, and *The New Gold Standard*.

"In this book, Howard Partridge shows us that the most important aspect of life is discovered by having correct insights into how life actually works. Much of it is found in understanding ourselves and other people who make up our own community. Every reader will experience personal growth and development from the excellent information contained in this personal book."

—Robert A. Rohm, Ph.D., President, Personality Insights, Inc.

"Howard Partridge is a game changer for businesspeople wanting to maximize growth. His new book, *The Power of Community*, provides essential steps to create a greater and more engaging team member experience that strengthens culture, accelerates performance, and elevates the customer experience. His insight is especially relevant for managing today's workforce."

 —Dave Anderson, President, LearnToLead,
  author, *Unstoppable*

"This wonderful book shows you how to encourage and inspire your people to put their whole hearts into your success."

 —Brian Tracy, author, *Full Engagement*

"Howard Partridge is a coach, mentor, and leader worth following. His contribution to empowering leaders to build community in their organizations has transformed many lives (my own included!) and has led to a community movement of its own through Howard's Inner Circle. The ideas shared in this book, when practiced, are transformative to the point that Ziglar, Inc., handpicked Howard to join the leadership team to help steer Mr. Zig Ziglar's legacy into the future."

 —Evan Desjardins, President, Ziglar, Inc.

"The power of community brings forth a simple but important idea . . . that community is vitally important in business. This book follows the principle of Givers Gain®, and I highly recommend it."

 —Ivan Misner, Ph.D., Founder, BNI

"What's missing in America today? We are all going our separate ways and we've lost touch with the power we possess together! In Howard's book, he does a masterful job of encouraging us to return to COMMUNITY. You will want to share this book with friends, family members, and coworkers. Thank you, Howard, for putting together a book that has the potential to bring us back to where we find our power—back to COMMUNITY!"

—Cheri Perry, President & Cofounder,
Total Merchant Concepts

The Power of Community an absolute must-read for anyone who leads a team—whether it's two or two hundred employees. Howard Partridge candidly describes, from personal experience, the incredible and dramatic difference that fostering a true sense of community among employees will make to a company's overall success. Get your highlighter ready—this book will become your reference manual for years to come!"

—Mark Timm, Executive Vice President, Ziglar, Inc., and
CEO, Ziglar Family

"Howard's new book, *The Power of Community*, addresses one of the most important but often neglected areas in the business world. The principles and concepts he writes about are applicable to anyone interested in having better relationships and experiencing genuine community and true success not only in business but in every area of life.

"In addition to being a master communicator, team builder, business coach, and consultant, Howard has a proven track record of using these lessons to build several companies. He shares from a wealth of personal experience but is also a diligent learner from many other successful leaders. I highly recommend his book to anyone who wants to grow and improve in these areas."

—Jerry Wiles, D.D., North America Regional Director,
International Orality Network, and President Emeritus,
Living Water International

"We wander around our city streets, airports, coffeehouses, schools, and businesses with our heads down, transfixed by our phones. We are substituting 'likes' for genuine human connection. Instead of conversing, debating, and persuading, we post wordy, ineffective rants on social media. We are virtually connected to more people than ever, and though the Internet has had a positive, world-flattening effect, it feels like we are becoming more and more isolated. And, for so many, less hopeful. So, thank you, Howard Partridge, for your inspiring and elegantly practical book. Howard suggests that our 'longing for belonging' can be satisfied by creating healthy communities. That resonates, right? Even better, Howard shares exactly HOW to do that, with simple systems, the right questions, and a whole lotta love. Looking for better relationships with your family, friends, team members, and customers? Read on! BONUS: Turns out a flourishing community is very, very good for your business's bottom line, too."

—Ellen Rohr, President, ZOOM DRAIN Franchising, LLC

The

POWER
of
COMMUNITY

The

POWER

of

COMMUNITY

How Phenomenal Leaders
Inspire Their Teams,
Wow Their Customers,
and Make Bigger Profits

HOWARD PARTRIDGE

NEW YORK   CHICAGO   SAN FRANCISCO   ATHENS
LONDON   MADRID   MEXICO CITY   MILAN
NEW DELHI   SINGAPORE   SYDNEY   TORONTO

1 2 3 4 5 6 7 8 9   QFR   22 21 20 19 18 17

ISBN: 978-1-260-11716-5
MHID: 1-260-11716-2

e-ISBN: 978-1-260-11717-2
e-MHID: 1-260-11717-0

Library of Congress Cataloging-in-Publication Data
Names: Partridge, Howard, author.
Title: The power of community : how phenomenal leaders inspire their teams,
    wow their customers, and make bigger profits / Howard Partridge.
Description: New York : McGraw-Hill, [2018]
Identifiers: LCCN 2017038809| ISBN 9781260117165 (alk. paper) | ISBN
    1260117162
Subjects: LCSH: Leadership. | Corporate culture. | Communities. |
    Organizational behavior.
Classification: LCC HD57.7 .P36565 2018 | DDC 658.4/092—dc23 LC record
available at https://lccn.loc.gov/2017038809

To Denise and Christian Partridge.
Thank you for your phenomenal love for me.
You are my community and have been with me
through all the ups and downs of life.
I love you both with all my heart, all my soul,
all my might; and I always will.

CONTENTS

FOREWORD

BY BRIAN TRACY, author of *Full Engagement! Inspire,*
Motivate, and Bring Out the Best in Your People

"Why are some companies more successful and profitable than others?"

Having studied thousands of companies around the globe for decades, I've found that the answer is simple: the best companies have the *best managers.* As a result, the best companies have the best people, and that means people who consistently outthink, outcompete, and outperform their competitors.

In your workplace today, the people around you do their jobs because they want to, not because they have to. They do their jobs well because they feel *internally* challenged and *externally* appreciated. People respect their jobs and treat their companies well because you respect them and you treat them well.

Your job is to create a work environment where the negative factors that detract from performance are taken away, the neutral factors that are the minimum essentials of a job are satisfied, and the motivators are maximized. In this environment, people will be internally motivated and stimulated to make the most valuable contribution to your company that they possibly can.

Here's a valuable lesson I learned many years ago: the way you treat people, what you say and do that affects them emotionally, is more important in bringing out the best in people than all the education, intelligence, or experience you might have at doing your job.

The best news of all is that because you are motivated and influenced by the same things other people are, you already know everything you need to know to become an outstanding manager. You already know how to unlock the potential of the people around you, how to build a peak performance team that delivers consistently high levels of results for your company. You just need to apply it.

The Power of Community will help you have a very successful organization.

ACKNOWLEDGMENTS

A person's community is a result of everything that has been planted in him or her since birth, so thank you to everyone who has supported me, encouraged me, and helped me stay accountable with who I am becoming.

This is my seventh published book, and I've written hundreds of articles and thousands of training documents over the years, but this is the first book of this stature. It was no easy feat. Therefore, I would like to acknowledge those who made this particular work possible.

The mission of creating community inside organizations has been resonating in my soul for many years. This message has been longing to be released since I first drew the dream with multicolored Sharpies on an artist's pad at Michael Gerber's *Dreaming Room* experience. The vision of people across the world engaging in small groups supporting one another, encouraging one another, and helping one another be accountable never left my imagination. The vision has become a reality in my world, and thanks to the following people, the message is now in your hands.

My phenomenal wife, Denise Partridge, who has shown me what true community is. Our phenomenal son, Christian Partridge, who helped me become a better father.

My phenomenal team that lives true community inside my companies.

Tom Ziglar for being a phenomenal champion connection for this work. You, your family, and those you have brought into my life have forever marked my heart.

Dr. Ralph Neighbor Jr. for your tireless work helping churches live out community around the world.

Bill Beckham for being my faithful mentor and showing me how to love others authentically.

Juanell Teague and Karyn Brownlee for the painstaking work you did to pull this message out of me.

Jodi Carroll for sharing your brilliant mind and beautiful heart. The countless conversations about community and life overwhelm me with gratitude.

Dr. Joseph A. Michelli for believing in me and introducing me to McGraw-Hill.

Donya Dickerson at McGraw-Hill for believing in the message before knowing the man.

Mark Ehrlich for being my tor-mentor in black.

Ellen Rohr for being a faithful and "funomenal" colleague.

Cheri Perry for becoming the champion of PODS.

Brenda Sell for sharing your community story for this book and your faithfulness in praying for me and the community.

The entire Howard Partridge Inner Circle Coaching Community for supporting me, encouraging me, and your love for one another. Your commitment is amazing.

The

POWER

of

COMMUNITY

INTRODUCTION:
A LONGING FOR
BELONGING

Every human being has a longing for belonging. We all want to feel loved, accepted, and validated. We want to feel that our lives matter. Deep down, we want to *belong* to something bigger than ourselves. We want to make a positive difference. Today, we are more connected digitally than ever before, yet we often feel more isolated and disconnected personally than ever.

This sense of isolation not only affects our personal lives but dramatically affects our work life as well. The ongoing Gallup Employee Engagement Poll* reveals that 70 percent of American workers are disengaged from their work. Perhaps even more disturbing, 18 percent of those workers are *actively* disengaged, meaning they are actually working *against* the success of the company. Not surprisingly, this lack of positive purpose bleeds over from employees to customers and has a serious negative impact on our organizations.

---

* http://news.gallup.com/poll/180404/gallup-daily-employee-engagement.aspx.

There is, however, one simple concept by which leaders can reengage their team members and transform their businesses to be phenomenally successful. That concept is *community*, and that's what *The Power of Community* is all about. This book will show you how to build a sense of community in your organization that not only will help you engage your team but will create more loyal and devoted clients in the process, which in turn will create higher returns for your organization.

Community has many meanings for many people. We often use it to refer to a neighborhood or local area, and we sometimes refer to an ethnic group as a community, but the kind of community we are talking about goes much deeper than just a neighborhood or a group of people. It's about the sense of belonging that all humans hunger for—the need to be connected to one another, the deep desire to be a part of something meaningful, something that makes a difference. This longing for belonging can have either positive or negative consequences. It is the reason people join clubs and do volunteer work, and it is also the reason people join gangs.

Our own families are the first communities we belong to, but the family community that existed (for some) in the premodern world seems to be much rarer now. Some may never have had the benefit of a loving community around them, and the idea of being deeply involved in our family members' lives, enjoying one another's successes, and enduring one another's failures seems to have largely disappeared.

Some argue whether this sense of community ever really existed. After all, every family has endured some kind of trouble. Divorce, scandal, addictions, and a variety of issues have plagued many families in the past. And of course, the entirety of human history is littered with injustices, whether it be slavery, war, or corruption.

However, many people felt a sense of community as they grew up. At one time, a child could walk the streets of New York City in relative safety. However, today, you wouldn't allow a 10-year-old to walk a block in most cities. Ironically, at the same time, our children are heavily influenced by a media of strangers lurking behind the screen they hold in their hand. Unfortunately, losing the sense of community in our culture has spilled over into virtually every other aspect of our lives, including our business lives. As a result, our organizations today mirror the detachment many feel.

Yet as we pursue our individual agendas, deep down we all long to experience community. And not only those of us who remember feeling a sense of community in the past yearn for it. Many of our younger people, today's new workforce, may never have felt this sense of belonging, but they long for it like everyone else. The need for community and connectedness is built into all humans.

A genuine community is a group of people who belong to one another. True community is a group of people who are committed to one another in every way possible. They share the same vision and values in life. They care for one another deeply. Someone you're in community with would get up in the middle of the night for you for any reason.

Social media gives us a sense of connectedness, but a "virtual community" is an oxymoron. True community requires the human touch. In the digital age, many young people have never felt true community or the love and encouragement that true community can bring. But they long for it. Everyone does. They may not know what to call it or even how to explain it, but the feeling is there. Like everyone else, they crave appreciation and recognition—even the number of likes and retweets on social media are important to them. Deep down, whether they know it or not, every human being wants to make a positive difference. We want our lives to matter. We all have a longing for belonging.

Business owners and managers who understand and implement the principles of building community within their organizations can help their team members experience a feeling of being truly connected and valued. A sense of being part of something bigger than themselves. In return, those employees will love being part of the company and will be more likely to treat others with respect and appreciation. That in turn will create loyal customers and, ultimately, bigger profits for the organization.

In order to help leaders achieve this goal, *The Power of Community* takes you through the process of building a sense of community in your organization both internally and externally.

You'll learn what phenomenal leaders do and how to create a rich environment of support, encouragement, and accountability that will inspire your team, "WOW" your customers, and make your organization bigger profits (Figure I.1).

THE THREE KEYS TO COMMUNITY
1. Support
2. Encouragement
3. Accountability

Figure I.1   The Three Keys to Community

You'll then learn the Six Steps to Building Community (Figure I.2) and what phenomenal leaders do to create community in their organizations:

1. **Value true community.** Phenomenal leaders *value* others.

2. **Pursue champion connections.** Phenomenal leaders *serve* others.

3. **Inspire emotional trust.** Phenomenal leaders *care for* others.

4. **Practice gift exchange.** Phenomenal leaders *develop* others.

5. **Invite openhearted encounters.** Phenomenal leaders *love* others.

6. **Build Growth PODS™.** Phenomenal leaders *coach* others.

THE SIX STEPS TO BUILDING A COMMUNITY

1. Value True Community

2. Pursue Champion Connections

3. Inspire Emotional Trust

4. Practice Gift Exchange

5. Invite Openhearted Encounters

6. Build Growth PODS

Figure I.2   The Six Steps to Building Community

Next, we will look at the building blocks for systematizing your community. Every tribe and every community has its "way" of doing things that must be identified and communicated by the leaders of the organization.

In this section, you'll learn the Five P's of Building Your Community System:

1. **Purpose.** Why your community exists.

2. **Positions.** The roles of the team members.

3. **PRD (Performance Results Descriptions).** What each team member is responsible for.

4. **Policies.** The rules of the game.

5. **Procedures.** The team playbook.

Finally, you'll discover how to create a meaningful community brand experience for your customer, client, patient, member, or guest that generates tremendous loyalty and an increased number of referrals.

As a business owner for over 33 years I've practiced these steps, and for over two decades I have helped small business owners around the world in hundreds of industries implement the principles outlined in this book with phenomenal success. This book offers practical, real-life examples that will enable you as a business owner or manager to understand what community really is and how it can be applied in your business or organization. But most important, it will show you how to reap the three big rewards of building community: inspired, engaged team members; happy, loyal clients; and increased, healthier profits.

WHY WE NEED COMMUNITY

CHAPTER 1

Have you ever been in the same room with someone who is plugged into his or her phone and not paying attention to you? Have you ever been that person?

I have.

Today, more than ever before, strangers on a screen influence people's minds, molding their beliefs, instilling fear rather than hope. Communication has been reduced to e-mails, instant messages, sound bites, and tweets.

Today, more than ever before, strangers on a screen influence people's minds, molding their beliefs, instilling fear rather than hope.

A couple of years ago, I was on the balcony of my hotel room in Clearwater Beach sipping a cup of coffee. Looking down from the tenth floor, I could see an employee of the hotel who was supposed to

7

be washing off the boardwalk with a garden hose. The reason I knew she was supposed to be doing that is there was a garden hose in her left hand with water coming out of it. But in her right hand was her phone, which she was much more interested in. Each time she looked at her phone to scroll, the garden hose strayed off course into the bushes rather than washing the sand off the walkway.

The challenge for leaders today is to make our work more compelling than whatever is happening in the media or what's happening on a team member's screen. That's a tall order and a big part of the reason we need a sense of community in our workplaces. Not that we can compete with a person's social connections or the seductive power of the media, but we can make our work so meaningful to our team members that they will engage at an unprecedented level. Building a sense of belonging—a sense of community—in our companies is the answer.

In the Introduction I mentioned the staggering employee engagement statistics. A study by psychologist Michelle McQuaid showed that many employees would pass on a 20 percent raise in order to get their boss *fired*!* That means that an employee making $30,000 per year is willing to give up *$6,000 every year* just to get rid of his or her manager.

Recently a Yelp employee's blog post went viral when she complained about not being able to pay her bills while the CEO made millions of dollars per year. Even though she got some deserved feedback about being more responsible, the fact is that she didn't *feel* cared for and felt the only way to vent her frustration was to post on her blog.

---

* Cited in Meghan Casserly, "Majority of Americans Would Rather Fire Their Boss Than Get a Raise," *Forbes*, October 17, 2012, https://www.forbes.com/sites/meghancasserly/2012/10/17/majority-of-americans-would-rather-fire-their-boss-than-get-a-raise/#1b1446c46610.

A few years ago, ABCs *20/20* did a special on how disgruntled employees quit their jobs in flamboyant ways. One hired a marching band to follow him into the manager's office and filmed the occasion. Another guy stood on a table in a crowded lunchroom and tugged his shirt open to reveal "I QUIT" marked on his chest with a big black marker.

Everyone cheered.

Although achieving true community in a company may seem unrealistic and maybe even unnecessary to you, the benefits of intentionally creating a *culture of community* that can lead to true community are worth pursuing. Having a team that is truly engaged and inspired can do wonders for any organization. An involved team will have less stress and conflict, and they will take great care of your clients, which in turn creates bigger profits for your organization.

Author Jim Collins observed that meaningful work equals a meaningful life. The reason we need community is to reengage our team members. It's the only weapon powerful enough to disrupt the digital disconnect that happens in every company today.

Meaningful work equals a meaningful life.

All leadership experts agree that culture is the most important thing in any business. This book is about defining your culture and creating a sense of belonging by creating a culture of community.

I've seen the benefits of this level of belonging in my own companies as well as my clients' companies around the world. It *can* be done, but it doesn't happen naturally. The only way to get there is to intentionally create it. It will be challenging, but it will be worth the effort, as you'll have something very few companies have.

The challenge when bringing people together in the world today is that each of us has different values, a different personality, and different ways of dealing with conflict. Each one of us has a different vision of the way work and life should be.

We have all learned different ways of communicating as we've grown up. For example, my wife is of Italian heritage from New Jersey. I'm a laid-back Southern boy originally from Alabama who moved to Texas at age 18. It was shocking for me to learn that family members could scream and shout at one another (as my wife's family might occasionally do) and still love each other.

Based on the way I was raised, I assumed that people who loved one another didn't have conflict. Everyone in my family did his or her "own thing," and if we disagreed with someone, we just stayed quiet about it. In that world, we never crossed one another.

Psychologists call this "fight or flight." My wife, Denise, is a *fighter*, and I grew up being a *flighter*. We had to learn how to communicate. Fortunately for us, our core values are the same and we have been happily married for 33 years.

Much like our marriage, your team members may come from different cultures and have different values. However, as the leader of the organization, you're responsible for creating the right environment for a sense of community to prosper.

Leadership Is Essential for Building Community

In order to transform your organization, you'll have to build a foundation on leadership. As leadership expert John Maxwell reminds us, "Everything rises and falls on leadership." Before leaders are able to change their culture to create community in their organization, they must first learn to be better leaders. Leadership is effectively communicating your vision. *Phenomenal* leadership is creating a community *experience* that inspires the team to implement. In order to accomplish that, leaders need two things: we must have a meaningful, compelling vision, and we must learn to communicate well.

Leadership is effectively communicating your vision.

In their phenomenal book *Beyond Entrepreneurship—Turning Your Business into an Enduring Great Company*, Jim Collins and the late William C. Lazier underscore the need for communication. They point out an unfortunate fact: many company leaders don't communicate. Not that they can't—they just don't. Collins and Lazier have a lot to say about vision, too (emphasis mine):

1. Vision forms the basis of extraordinary human effort.

2. Vision provides a context for strategic and tactical decisions.

3. Shared vision creates cohesion, teamwork, and *community*.

4. Vision lays the groundwork for the company to evolve past dependence on a few key individuals.

Finally, they say that "to become great, . . . a company must progress past excessive dependence on one or a few key individuals. The vision must become *shared as a community*."

Every team needs a compelling vision. Too many organizations have a vision statement that was cooked up in an off-site leadership retreat but has no real meaning to the team. Some companies even frame their vision statement and proudly hang it on the wall in the lobby. The problem is that not even the receptionist, who sits 10 feet away from it every day, could tell you what is says, much less what it means. Or more important, what it has to do with him or her personally. There is no connection with how it affects the individual lives of the team.

Even when leaders have a clear vision, the more difficult part is *communicating* that vision to the team. We seem to have difficulty communicating effectively today. For one thing, technology continues to change how we communicate with one another. Or better said, how we *attempt* to communicate. The digital age has created a false sense of connection that has fostered the separateness many feel—even though there is something wonderful about a soldier across the world being able to see his baby being born via Skype.

Along with rapid changes in technology, there are also differences in how millennials and baby boomers communicate. Older people may prefer to talk over the phone, whereas younger people prefer to text.

Personality styles come into play as well. We are all wired a little differently and therefore communicate differently. Many different religious and family values exist in today's workplace and also play a part in the communication gap. All of us hear with a different set of ears, and we see with different-colored glasses.

Community is the answer to bringing together all these diverse types of people, as it is the ultimate form of communication. Leadership can communicate most effectively in the context of community. When a group of people feel like they belong to one another, they feel cared for, and they believe that the vision is worth sacrificing for, they will go the extra mile for the company. There's no stopping a group of people who not only have the same vision and values but feel like they belong to one another—and know their team has their back.

If you think about the word *community* for a moment, it really means "communicating in unity." John Maxwell wrote a book titled *Everyone Communicates, Few Connect*. Communicating is just one part of the equation. Unity is the other part. It's only when we are truly connecting that we're really unified. Or better put—when we're unified, we connect better.

A few years ago, as a participant in John Maxwell's highest-level leadership group, Exchange, I sat with the group in a Delta Airlines hangar as John interviewed Ed Bastian, CEO of Delta Airlines. Little did we know that the "surprise experience" that is always a part of Exchange would have us boarding a chartered jet to fly us from Atlanta to the Country Music Hall of Fame in Nashville to hear radio celebrity Dave Ramsey speak.

Dave Ramsey is a business owner and leader who has built a phenomenal culture of community among his 500+ person company. One reason his team members have unity is that they communicate regularly. Every Monday morning the entire group has a huddle for an hour. Many of them are paid by the hour, so you can imagine what the weekly investment is for that meeting. You'll find, I stress throughout this book, that there is no escaping meeting on a regular basis when you're building a team or a community. You cannot communicate effectively if you avoid meetings.

In Nashville that night, Dave shared what he called the Five Enemies of Unity:

1. Poor communication

2. Gossip

3. Unresolved disagreements

4. Lack of shared purpose

5. Sanctioning incompetence

When team members feel a sense of community, everyone has shared goals and shared values. When that happens, everyone is pulling in the same direction, getting more done. When the team is free from the friction that comes from hidden agendas, backstabbing, and outright lies that often exist in the corporate world, team members will tend to be more open, honest, and engaged, and therefore more productive.

That doesn't mean there won't be conflict. Just like in any loving family, there will be disagreements and even healthy arguments. When you get any group of human beings together, there will be conflict. As Dave Ramsey also likes to say, "Leadership is easy—until people get involved." In any group of people, false assumptions can be made about intentions, but when we know we can trust one another and that we are all after the same goal, we can engage in *healthy* conflict. Without regular communication we won't have unity.

Author Patrick Lencioni, a highly respected and sought after leadership expert with immense experience in organizational development, declares in his book *The Five Dysfunctions of a Team*, "Not finance. Not strategy. Not technology. It is teamwork that remains the ultimate competitive advantage, both because it is so powerful and so rare."

The five dysfunctions of a team that Lencioni describes in his book are:

1. Absence of trust

2. Fear of conflict

3. Lack of commitment

4. Avoidance of accountability

5. Inattention to results.

And in his book *The Advantage: Why Organizational Health Trumps Everything Else in Business*, Patrick takes it a step further by proclaiming that "organizational health" is the ultimate competitive advantage.

He writes that an organization that is healthy has minimal politics, minimal confusion, high morale, high productivity, and low turnover and says, "Once organizational health is properly understood and placed into the right context, it will surpass all other disciplines in business as the greatest opportunity for improvement and competitive advantage." He even maintains that organizational health is, "far bigger and more important than mere culture."

Organizational health, Patrick says, "is about making a company function effectively by building a cohesive leadership team, establishing real clarity among those leaders, communicating that clarity to everyone within the organization and putting in place just enough structure to reinforce that clarity going forward" (https://www.table group.com/organizational-health).

Again, leadership is *effectively communicating* your vision. Bill Beckham, one of my early mentors, taught me that "vision + vision = division." When two people on a team have different visions, agendas soon develop, and if those visions are not reconciled, the team becomes divided on issues.

My contention is that building community is the next step beyond organizational health. Healthy communication is the first level, belonging is the second, and true community is the ultimate level. This book will help you establish a vision for your organization, and more important, it will help you communicate that vision more effectively. Hopefully to the point that you and your team can enjoy a culture of genuine community.

As you move toward that end, you can reap the associated benefits:

- A happy, engaged, inspired team

- Happy, devoted, loyal customers

- Bigger, healthier profits

How Community Changed My Life

Several years ago, I would go to church every Sunday, and although the sermon was nice—and sometimes even really meaningful—something was missing. There didn't seem to be any real life change. It was *stale* religion.

This book isn't about church or religion but what happened to me that became instructive in business: On Tuesday nights we had home group in which a small band of church members met at someone's home, and we sat in a circle. Kenny played the guitar. Jim was collecting money to help someone fix her car. Elise was baby-sitting my son in the other room.

Real ministry was happening. One had a prayer, one had a song, and one had a message. This group *belonged* to one another. This was true community. It was "rare air." Unfortunately, many businesses have gone stale and don't enjoy this feeling of belonging. We go through the motions, but the joy and fulfillment of interacting with one another seems to be missing. Work has become meaningless, and when that happens, team members become disengaged.

We talk a lot from the front of the room, send a plethora of e-mails, write memos, and have lots of meetings, but it's mostly a one-way conversation. Many leaders do a poor job of communicating.

Don't get me wrong—large group meetings are important to inspire and to teach, and of course memos and messages are important, too, but if leaders want their employees to implement their ideas, they need to go deeper. If we want meaningful engagement that turns into massive implementation, we need a sense of belonging—a sense of community. And that happens most effectively in *small groups*.

Someone once quipped, "We learn in rows, but we grow in circles." Small groups are the key building blocks in establishing community. In this book, I will introduce you to a simple process I call Growth PODS. Growth PODS are small groups that typically include seven to nine individuals and are designed to support, encourage, and hold participants accountable to do the things they need to do and to help people become the persons they need to be. PODS stands for Power of Discovery Systems. Participants "discover" what they need to do (or how they need to act) rather than being taught—or worse, *told*. Essentially, Growth PODS are a way of organizing team members that allows them to open up about issues in a nonthreatening way.

PODS can be used to address both personal and professional issues, including reaching personal goals, changing habits, or developing one's skills, as well as reaching company goals, keeping a project moving forward, or creating new ideas. Establishing these groups throughout an organization contributes to creating a community-oriented atmosphere that, in turn, makes it possible to develop true community over time.

I've observed over the last three decades that something amazing happens when people come together in person, face-to-face, in small groups that are properly facilitated. Personal interaction without hiding behind a screen can facilitate real connection, which over time can grow into a sense of community. Community happens most effectively in a small group setting, so if you have a large company, you'll want to start a POD with your core leadership team first. Then, by multiplying your groups, you can create a sense of community companywide regardless of how large your organization is. I'll show you how later in this book.

The question for now is, How did we lose the sense of community many once felt in our society? And why is that important? Understanding what can take away the sense of community is vital to reestablishing it. In order to change the future, many times you need to know what happened in the past. History tends to repeat itself unless we are diligent to change it.

In the next chapter, we will review the events of history that led to the lack of community many seem to feel today.

HOW WE LOST OUR SENSE OF COMMUNITY

Several years ago I was visiting some friends in Costa Rica. I had helped support their church there for quite some time, and they wanted me to come and meet the congregation. As I visited individual church members in their homes, I noticed more and more televisions had appeared in each home compared with when I was there a few years earlier. When I spoke to the congregation, I encouraged them not to copy *all* the ways of the postmodern world. I shared with them that they still had the one thing people in more developed countries longed for—genuine community.

Before the turn of the twentieth century, people had to rely on one another to get along in life. Yet today many of us don't even know our next-door neighbor. We use GPS on our phones for directions, the Internet to buy and deliver anything needed, and Google for any fact we need to know.

A television commercial for a major rental care company expresses a common attitude of our postmodern culture. Patrick John Warburton (best known for his character Puddy in the television show

Seinfeld) enters the scene bragging about being a control "enthusiast" and announces that at National, he can bypass the counter and he doesn't even have to talk to "any humans" unless he wants to. As he walks by and goes straight to his car, two pleasant-looking National employees stand by smiling, at his service, just in case he needs something. Of course he doesn't even acknowledge their presence.

As someone who travels often, I'll be the first to admit that I'm a little miffed when there is an error with my Gold Service and I have to wait in a line rather than going directly to my rental car. The benefit of the convenience is not in question here. It's the question of how we are relating to one another and what's happening to our connectedness to one another.

Today, the digital revolution is paving the way for complete isolation and reliance on machines rather than human interaction. The problem is that you can't have a real relationship with a machine. Have you heard of the Japanese pop star Hatsune Miku? She has two and a half million Facebook fans, has over 255,000 YouTube subscribers, and has performed on late night television shows. The surprising part? She's not even real. She's a holographic image.

Artificial intelligence is creating lifelike robots that we can control through an app. What happened to humans that we couldn't satisfy one another any longer? IBM's Watson may be intelligent, but "he" can't build an authentic relationship. What happened to the sense of community we once felt? This change wasn't brought on by any one specific event but, rather, by a series of events that occurred over many years.

Gutenberg to Zuckerberg

Obviously our world has been changing rapidly for centuries. Gutenberg's invention of the printing press created a huge shift. Here's how

Wikipedia describes the impact in its article on Johannes Gutenberg: "[Gutenberg's] introduction of mechanical movable type printing to Europe started the Printing Revolution and is widely regarded as the most important invention of the second millennium, the seminal event which ushered in the modern period of human history."

There was another major shift at the beginning of the twentieth century when, for the first time in human history, more of the world's population lived in cities than in rural communities. As the locomotive and the automobile became a part of normal life, the Industrial Revolution steamed forward.

The factory, rather than the family farm, became the "normal" workplace, which brought tough management systems. As strangers worked next to one another, they became just another cog in the wheel of industry. "Command and control" management was the order of the day during the Industrial Revolution. Then came the airplane, the telephone, and the television. Here's a story that shares the sentiment many people feel today . . .

The Stranger—Author Unknown

A few months before I was born, my dad met a stranger who was new to our small Tennessee town. From the beginning, Dad was fascinated with this enchanting newcomer and soon invited him to live with our family. The stranger was quickly accepted and was around to welcome me into the world a few months later.

As I grew up I never questioned his place in our family. Mom taught me to love the Word of God. Dad taught me to obey it. But the stranger was our storyteller. He could weave the most fascinating tales. Adventures, mysteries and comedies were daily conversations. He could hold our whole family spellbound for hours each evening.

He was like a friend to the whole family. He took Dad, Bill, and me to our first major league baseball game. He was always encouraging us to see the movies and he even made arrangements to introduce us to several movie stars.

The stranger was an incessant talker. Dad didn't seem to mind, but sometimes Mom would quietly get up—while the rest of us were enthralled with one of his stories of faraway places—and go to her room read her Bible and pray. I wonder now if she ever prayed that the stranger would leave. You see, my dad ruled our household with certain moral convictions. But this stranger never felt an obligation to honor them. Profanity, for example, was not allowed in our house—not from us, from our friends, or adults. Our longtime visitor, however, used occasional four-letter words that burned my ears and made Dad squirm. To my knowledge the stranger was never confronted.

My dad was a teetotaler who didn't permit alcohol in his home—not even for cooking. But the stranger felt he needed exposure and enlightened us to other ways of life. He offered us beer and other alcoholic beverages often. He made cigarettes look tasty, cigars manly, and pipes distinguished.

He talked freely (much too freely) about sex. His comments were sometimes blatant, sometimes suggestive, and generally embarrassing. I know now that my early concepts of the man/woman relationship were influenced by the stranger. As I look back, I believe it was the grace of God that the stranger did not influence us more.

Time after time he opposed the values of my parents. Yet he was seldom rebuked and never asked to leave. More than thirty years have passed since the stranger moved in with the young family on Morningside Drive. But if I were to walk into my parents' den today, you would still see him sitting over in a corner, waiting for someone to listen to him talk and watch him draw his pictures.

His name? We always called him TV.

I'm certainly not against technology, but it's worth recognizing that if we are going to truly connect with and care for those we live and work with each day, we're going to have to be intentional about how we use our technology and how we connect with one another. In order to create a sense of community that will engage your team, it's important to understand how our digital world has come to command our lives and keep us from connecting authentically.

In the 1960s there was another major shift. Data clearly shows a direct correlation between the rise of technology and the decline of face-to-face social groups.

In the year 2000, in his three-inch-thick book *Bowling Alone— The Collapse and Revival of American Community*, Robert D. Putnam warns that our stock of social capital—the very fabric of our connections with one another—has plummeted, impoverishing our lives and communities.

Putnam draws on evidence including nearly 500,000 interviews over the last quarter century to show that we sign fewer petitions, belong to fewer organizations that meet, know our neighbors less, meet with friends less frequently, and even socialize with our families less often. We're even bowling alone. He found that more people are bowling than ever before, but they are not bowling in leagues. Putnam shows how changes in work, family structure, age, suburban life, television, computers, women's roles, and other factors have contributed to this decline.

Putnam writes, "Over the last three decades a variety of social, economic, and technological changes have rendered obsolete a significant stock of America's social capital. Television, two-career families, suburban sprawl, generational changes and values—these and other changes in American society have meant that fewer and fewer of us find that the League of Women Voters, or the United Way, or the Shriners, or the monthly bridge club, or even a Sunday picnic with friends fits the way we have come to live. Our growing social-capital deficit threatens educational performance, safe neighborhoods, equitable tax collection, democratic responsiveness, everyday honesty, and even our health and happiness."

Live television brought Watergate, the Vietnam War, and the assassinations of JFK and MLK into our living rooms. A media of strangers began to instill fear rather than hope into our lives on a massive scale. Not that the influence wasn't already there with newspaper and radio. But television became the new baby-sitter. Born in 1960, I recall occasionally falling asleep in front of the television as the national anthem closed the broadcasting for the night.

Today, we live in an extraordinary time, when a 10-year-old has access to every kind of influence imaginable behind a screen but can't walk down the street in safety. We cannot change that, but we *can* change how we manage our relationships. How can we best manage relationships in this digital age?

Recently, I was attending a conference and the keynote speaker, a social media celebrity and digital marketer, was sharing how he is heavily investing in virtual reality because it's the next "big thing." During the Q&A session, I asked him, "If it's true that people have a longing for belonging, and deep down, they *crave* true community, how does virtual reality coexist with that truth?" He responded with, "Howard, I think people *do* want that real connection, but VR tricks the human mind and changes people's state. It's just a fact."

Artificial intelligence is another trend that promises lifelike companionship with a machine. Machines give humans extraordinary experiences, but nothing can replace a real relationship. The concern here is that the more accustomed we become to relating to images on screens, in "virtual" environments, and soon with artificial beings, the farther we move from real community. A virtual community is an oxymoron. We are reaching out to machines because we are starving for real connections. How do we get meaning out of life when machines do all of our work and all of our connecting? We seem to view that scenario as Utopia.

Phenomenal Leaders Build
Real Relationships

The key to community is to be intentional about investing in others and building meaningful relationships. My experience is that understanding and engaging in true community will give you the richest experience you've ever encountered. But it won't be easy.

Community cannot be forced. Building community is messy because you're dealing with flawed human beings. You'll sometimes fail in the process of trying to connect with people and especially trying to connect them to one another. You'll probably get hurt, and others may get hurt in the process.

The idea of living, learning, and loving together will not be easy. As we have all learned, love hurts, but it's the only way. The good news is that building a sense of belonging in your organization, although not easy, is very simple.

All of business and all of life is about relationships. Phenomenal leaders understand that humans are starving for authentic relationships. In their classic leadership book *The Leadership Challenge: How to Make Extraordinary Things Happen in Organizations*, legendary leadership authors James M. Kouzes and Barry M. Posner describe leadership as a *relationship*. It's the quality of this relationship that matters most when people are engaged in getting extraordinary things done. "A leader-constituent relationship characterized by fear and distrust will never produce anything of lasting value. A relationship characterized by mutual respect and confidence will overcome the greatest adversities and leave a legacy of significance."

Phenomenal leaders understand that humans are starving for authentic relationships.

At one of my conferences, my colleague Ellen Rohr was teaching from the stage on leadership. She asked the audience what some of their leadership challenges were. A guy in the audience complained that his employee wanted to be his friend. "Oh, that's *terrible!*" Ellen teased with her boisterous, in-your-face style. "I can't imagine anything worse than that!" she exclaimed.

Why is it that leaders and managers avoid having a relationship with team members? Many business owners and leaders worry that if they get too close to their employees, they will be taken advantage of. They fear the employee will fail to perform and will expect leniency. Although that is certainly a possibility—and I have personally had that happen to me—the instructions in this book will help you build a meaningful personal relationship while maintaining a strong professional relationship. Most people haven't learned how to be authentic with one another and therefore have not been able to maintain the balance between the two. This is a relationship skill that can be developed. It is abundantly clear that when there is at minimum a relationship of mutual respect and trust, more can be accomplished. I seek to take leaders even beyond that point.

What's the alternative? To work side by side with people you don't know anything about? To spend the majority of your waking hours with people you don't trust and maybe even despise? This is precisely the problem in many workplaces today. We don't trust the person next to us, mainly because we don't *know* him or her. Or maybe it's because the leader hasn't created the right environment for healthy relationships to prosper. Phenomenal leaders understand that leadership is a *relationship*.

Positive relationships are built on trust and respect. As you'll discover in this book, before we care for something, we have to value it. Before we respect someone, we must value that person. This is why the first step in building community is valuing people. Not for what they've done, but for who they are. Human beings have inherent value and should be respected and dignified for that.

Positive relationships are built on trust and respect.

Whether you can work together with team members will depend on your ability to build healthy relationships. You'll also discover how you can build strong relationships while avoiding the expectation of special favors. In fact, if you build community the right way, your team members will be eager to work with you and will be interested in you reaching your goals and interested in doing all that is possible to help you have the life you want. I know, because that is my reality every day, and I'm helping others do the same. I'll end this chapter with two examples. The first is from one of our coaching clients, Cheri Perry. Cheri and her husband, Dean, own a credit card processing company in Vancouver, Washington. Cheri says:

> Running a business can be hard work—in fact, it can zap the very life out of you. If you're not careful, it can literally change you from being a DREAM chaser to a dollar chaser—and that dark transformation was exactly why I found myself looking for something . . . turns out that something was COMMUNITY.

When I first met Howard Partridge, my company was doing fine. We had the same issues that every business has involving employees and disengagement and I was constantly seeking ways to help the staff become better, more efficient, more effective. We had a decent culture, but that something extra was missing. As I watched Howard's team and how they LOVED him and poured into his clients, I began to experience COMMUNITY and realized that the little extra that I'd been looking for had to begin with ME. Where does community start—turns out the answer is—in the mirror. Instead of seeking ways to fix my team, I began to look for ways to change my perspective and add value to my team.

Howard and I were introduced through our common friend Zig Ziglar, so it is no surprise that Zig's quote: "You can have everything in life you want if you just help enough other people get what they want," is one that we both love. In order to help others get what they want, you have to KNOW what they want, and that is where my company was missing the boat. I loved my team but I had not taken the time to really dig in and find out how I could help them get what they wanted! Community implies knowing each other and so I got busy.

Today, we have created a beautiful community at work, and it has made all the difference. We still have all the elements and some of the challenges associated with any business environment, but the community we have crafted together has helped us take our game to the next level.

- We used to be irritated when people brought their personal lives into work . . . today we look for ways to help.

- We used to focus solely on business goals . . . today every staff member has a vision board and is assisted in achieving their personal goals.

- We used to expect people to fit into a certain mold . . .
  today we accept people as they are and help them become
  their best.

- We used to focus on selling accounts . . . today we focus
  on adding value to our prospects & clients.

Community used to be just another word for me—today it is
everything. It is the path to fulfillment, success, belonging, and
yes—even greater success financially. When we truly care about
those people we interact with: our team, our clients, and our referral partners, we create a community, and there is PEOPLE
POWER in a community. I am so thankful for Howard and his team
for inviting us into their community and helping us strengthen our
own in the process.

The second example comes from a coaching client, senior grand-
master Brenda J. Sell, who is a ninth degree black belt, a world title
holder, and president of U.S. Chung Do Kwan Association, Inc.
Brenda wrote:

50 years ago our business began in an old renovated laundro-
mat that was turned into our first school for America's oldest
Taekwondo association, the United States Chung Do Kwan Association. Our business was built on the premise that those enrolled
in our Taekwondo classes would benefit personally and develop
into leaders who would make a positive difference in their communities. This would require many hard lessons in developing
what we now call "community."

In the early days, the saying was "don't fraternize with the
students"—in other words, keep business strictly business, and
don't cross the lines! Fear was a motivating factor, and my late
husband led with a hammer fist. Students would drop out quickly,

and only the strong survived. At first this was like a badge of honor. After losing 80% of our students, he decided it was time to regroup and create a different business model.

We maintained the highest caliber of training and credentials, while adding something unheard-of in martial arts at the time: relationships. Developing leaders became the priority. People knew it was going to be tough, but they also knew they were loved, appreciated, and valued. Incentives, rewards, and recognition were built into our training system. Small groups were formed to provide specialized training in leadership and character development. Events and social activities were added that build lifelong relationships with us and each other. We share the same vision. Today, 50 years later, we have members who are still connected from 40–45 years ago! Howard says, "Community is a place where people know each other deeply, serve each other willingly, celebrate each other enthusiastically, and mourn the setbacks in life together. It's a place characterized by genuine care and concern for each member of the team." I've found this to be true.

In a matter of 15 months, I faced a series of "nightmare circumstances." My husband of 41 years passed away, I became the primary caregiver of my father, my mother became ill and is in a nursing home permanently, my dad passed, and I was diagnosed with breast cancer facing a year of treatment!

We have nearly 100 Taekwondo schools throughout America that we train, credential, and care for. During these difficult times, we did not lose one school. We mourned together, we supported each other and inspired each other. Because of my treatment for breast cancer, I was not able to maintain my day to day duties. New leaders rose up to carry on the vision and legacy. We hung onto the vision together and even added a few schools to our membership. We've expanded our leadership base and are empowering our team by equipping them with the tools they need to grow and expand.

To build community, you must believe in others, see the best in them, help them to identify with their gifts and talents, place them in the right positions, recognize their accomplishments, and guide them through challenges they will face. People need people. That's how we were designed.

These examples show that creating a sense of community is possible. In the next chapter, you'll learn the three keys that can unlock community in your organization and six concrete steps you can follow to take the sense of community to the next level.

THREE KEYS THAT UNLOCK TRUE COMMUNITY

Before reaching the ultimate goal of true community, you'll first need to create a sense of belonging, which can lead to a sense of community. Your first goal is simply to get your team members feeling like they belong to something meaningful rather than just going to a job every day.

As you, the leader, move through the Six Steps to Building Community and invite others to participate, you'll begin to grow together with true community as the ultimate goal. In the past, the best examples of this kind of community were strong, functional family units.

These families experienced community because they exhibited the three keys to creating *true* community—support, encouragement, and accountability. That is, they supported one another's goals, encouraged one another's gifts, and held each other accountable for maintaining the family's values.

Support is helping others have the life they want to have, and it's getting the help you need to have the things you want in life and in business. *Encouragement* is helping others find the courage to do the things they want to do and finding the courage yourself to do the things you find difficult to do. *Accountability* is giving others the feedback they need to become the persons they need or want to be, and it's getting the feedback you need to be the person you want to be.

For example, if a member of the family had a goal to build something, other family members might get involved to help. If one of them had some kind of difficulty, another family member was likely to provide encouragement by trying to cheer the person up. And if someone got into some kind of trouble, the other members of the family would provide advice or discipline—depending on which was appropriate—and the individual would in all likelihood accept it.

It seems like many families live such individual lives today. Family members seem to be spread so thin that it's difficult to be deeply involved in one another's lives as we pursue our individual agendas. This lack of true community in families is reflected in our workplaces. But if we understand and implement these three keys—in our families, among our friends, and in the workplace—we can begin the process of building community in our companies.

These three keys are not difficult to understand, but it is essential that we learn how to apply them if we want to achieve the three major benefits of developing community within our companies: an inspired, engaged team; happy, loyal customers; and bigger profits.

How the Three Keys Operate in Your Organization

The three keys look like this in a business environment—the Six Steps to Building Community are outlined with two steps under each key.

1. **Support.** Helping your team members reach their goals and realize their dreams. Step 1 is Value True Community, and Step 2 is Pursue Champion Connections.

2. **Encouragement.** Inspiring your team members to do the things they may be afraid to do. This key unlocks Step 3: Inspire Emotional Trust and Step 4: Practice Gift Exchange.

3. **Accountability.** Providing feedback to your team members so they can become the persons they need to be. The third key brings us to Step 5: Invite Openhearted Encounters and Step 6: Build Growth PODS.

Notice that the first step is to help your team members reach their goals. This is the key that starts the right kind of relationship that can then move toward the right culture, creating a sense of belonging. Eventually it can lead to a true sense of community.

If you want to create a supportive environment in your company, you have to be the example. If you want to get support, you have to give support. I was walking among the crowd at one of my conferences teaching on this subject, and a first-time attendee, who did not know me very well, blurted out, "Don't they have to earn *my* respect before I give *them* respect?" "No." I responded. "Exactly the opposite. Show them that you respect them first, and they will be more likely to respect you."

You'll find out that this process starts with how you value others. Leadership expert John Maxwell says, "Leadership is influence. Nothing more. Nothing less." He goes on to say that the way we gain influence in someone else's life is to add value to that person. When you don't value people, you de-value people.

When you believe in people, you are more likely to invest in building relationships with them. Many leaders simply see employees as a resource—maybe even a necessary evil—rather than as living, breathing, feeling human beings.

Community requires care. Good leaders care about others. If you don't care about others, they won't care about you. And if you care about someone, you'll value him or her. If you value people, you'll invest time, money, and resources supporting them. Support is the first key to establishing a sense of community in your organization.

Community requires care. Good leaders care about others.

I love the word *communicare*. We communicate because we care. Notice how the word is associated with the word *community*:

> The English term *communication* . . . evolved from [the] Latin language. *Communis* and *communicare* are two Latin words related to the word *communication*. *Communis* is [a] noun . . . which means "common, communality or sharing." Similarly, *communicare* is a verb, which means "make something common." Some scholars relate the term *communication* with [the] English word *community*. Community members have something common to each other. Communities are [supposed to be] formed with the tie of communication. It is the foundation of community. Hence, where there is no communication, there can't be a community. ("Origin of the Word," January 16, 2011, http://nepalicommunication .blogspot.com/2011/01/origin-of-word.html.)

When there is no *care*, there can't be community. When leaders value human beings as living, breathing, feeling, special creations rather than a human resource, they are more likely to invest in people. When we value something, we invest in it, and we protect it. When you help your team members reach their goals, both personally and professionally, they will help the company reach its goals.

Kevin Turner, former COO of Microsoft, said the first thing he asks someone who is joining his team is to share his or her goals and dreams. The late Zig Ziglar, an American legend and inspirational teacher, famously stated, "You can have everything in life you want, if you just help enough other people get what they want."

The First Key: Support

The first step in building community in your business is supporting your team members. Many employees feel that no one cares about them. What if you started helping your team members reach their goals in life? This is a major key to the whole idea of community. In order to get support, we have to give support.

Support is important because no one succeeds alone. We all need others to help us reach our goals and dreams. Of course, as a business leader, you want your company to be successful. But the ultimate benefit of that success is that it will enable *you* to achieve *your* personal life goals, which is why you started your business or took on your current leadership position in the first place. In order to achieve that success for yourself, you need the support of a team—not just your employees but also mentors, coaches, peers, vendors, and clients.

The only way to *get* support is by *giving* support. In order to do that, as the leader, you must take the first step. Many employees are disengaged and discouraged because they don't believe their organization really cares about them. Of course at a minimum, employees must have the tools and resources they need to accomplish the vision of the company, including the training they need to do their jobs well.

But they also need mentoring and coaching to understand and live out the company's visions and values. If you are genuinely interested in building community in your organization, it's even more important that you really get to know your employees, that you go the extra mile by making the effort to understand them and their goals and helping them reach those goals.

You may not be able to help your employees get *everything* they want, but imagine the difference it will make if they believe you are genuinely interested in them. By supporting them—by going the extra mile to help them reach their personal goals—you'll earn their support in your efforts to reach the goals of the organization.

The term "go the extra mile" was coined in Roman times. When requested, a Roman citizen was required to carry a soldier's gear for a mile. Most citizens would count off exactly one mile and drop the pack at exactly that spot. But others were willing to go further. Thus, "going the extra mile" became a metaphor for showing someone you care about him or her by doing more than what is expected.

What do you think happened in the soldiers' minds when a person went the "extra mile"? When soldiers saw the other persons care for them and their mission, they became much more interested in them.

This does, of course, go against the traditional approach to running a business today. Many leaders feel that all you have to do is get the right people with the right technical skills and everything else will take care of itself. The problem with that kind of thinking is that it doesn't work.

Hiring talented people has to be your first priority, but a collection of talented people is not a community. It's not even a team. Microsoft has 50,000 employees, but Kevin Turner understood the value of getting to know the people on his team. In fact, he has all new hires do a 30-minute "Who Am I" presentation in which they share information about where they are from, their families, their aspirations, and their strengths.

Hiring talented people has to be your first priority, but a collection of talented people is not a community.

The team members in my own companies are highly engaged because we show them that we care about them in a variety of ways. We start, of course, by providing them with the training they need to do their jobs. But we also go the extra mile for them. For example, during our training sessions, rather than simply focusing on technical training, we help them learn life skills, such as goal setting, as well as leadership training.

But we don't only help them set goals; when we can, we help them attain those goals. For example, they might want to write a book, go to college, or develop a healthier lifestyle. Once we find out what they want to achieve, we're always on the lookout for information, contacts, and resources that might help them do it. That not only benefits the company and the team members, it makes them grateful to the company for helping them grow. As a result, they display the kind of loyalty that most leaders never see.

Not surprisingly, because we do go the extra mile for our employees, they are willing to go the extra mile for the company. Our experience in building community is not, however, an isolated example. When I recently went to visit one of my clients who had implemented the keys to building community in his own organization and asked how strong the community was, he said, "Off the charts." And it was true! Walking around his offices, I saw a group of really engaged people who were both highly productive and highly supportive of one another and the company.

During the four days I stayed with him I attended several outside functions in which many of the employees were participants. And it was obvious that they supported one another, encouraged one another, and held one another accountable. When I asked my client how this came about, his response was simply, "We do life together." In other words, not only does this approach work, it works phenomenally well.

Step 1: Value True Community

The first step in the process of building community in an organization is to value true community, which means making it your top priority and acting accordingly. You can't just say that you value community; you have to show you value others, because if you don't set an example for your team, no one else will. When you value something, you give it attention and care; you cherish it, protect it, and develop it. And it's only by doing that, by practicing the three keys and making sure your team sees you do it, that you will be able to start building community in your company.

One example of how I've practiced this in my own organization was with my protégé Santiago Arango. He came from a wealthy family in Colombia but due to the drug cartel and political situation there had to flee to the United States, leaving everything behind. He started in one of my companies at an entry-level position at the age of 17, and I noticed early on that he was very talented and could be a real asset to the organization. I became his mentor, investing in him personally and emotionally, and now he works with me to train small business owners and their team members.

There was a moment when I was able to support Santiago in a very specific way. The day he became a U.S. citizen I made sure I was at the ceremony, after which we went to a local restaurant to celebrate. It was a special moment. True community is built through these kinds of experiences.

Step 2: Pursue Champion Connections

All of business is about relationships. In order to win in business, you need people around you whom you can trust. Every leader needs an inner circle of people who can provide mutual friendship by building winning relationships. As William A. Beckham points out, "Community begins with friendship." It begins with one friend, then two. A small group community emerges from there.

In order to win in business, you need faithful friends. You gain such friends by placing a very high value on people in your team. You see them as friends rather than as a human resource. Support them by helping them reach their goals in life, and they will support you.

Owners and managers need help from others as well. In fact, every successful individual has mentors, coaches, consultants, and associates who support him or her. As is the case with employees, the way to get support from these individuals is by first giving them support. Once you find people who have the same values you do and provide them with support, they are likely to support you in return. This step, pursue champion connections, is about making efforts to invest in relationships that have the potential of developing into strong alliances.

I've made this kind of investment many times in my life and can tell you that the benefits of doing so are greater than you can imagine. For example, for as long as I can remember, I admired the work of the legendary Zig Ziglar, one of the most popular inspirational figures of our time. Through his 36 books and thousands of speeches, it is estimated that he touched a quarter of a billion lives, and mine was one of them. He passed away in 2012, but before he did, I intentionally pursued a relationship with him. Having heard that his organization was always interested in finding new distributors for its products, I made an appointment with Margaret Garrett, who was a sales representative at Ziglar. During our meeting, she sensed that my values matched theirs and introduced me to Zig's son, CEO Tom Ziglar. Before the meeting was over, I had agreed to sell Ziglar products to my audience, and they had agreed that Zig would appear in person at my conference in Houston, which he did.

After that conference I continued to build a relationship with the Ziglar organization by visiting Tom at his office to talk about ways I could support them. I helped them get Zig's message out by inviting Tom and Julie (Zig's daughter) to speak at another one of my conferences. As a result of providing that support, I got to help Tom with the last chapter of Zig's last book, *Born to Win*.

In 2012, Tom asked me to be the exclusive business coach for Ziglar's small business customers, and I became the world's first Ziglar Legacy Certified Trainer. Tom and I now travel the world together helping small business owners transform their lives by building a better business. This all came about by simply following Zig's philosophy, "You can have everything in life you want, if you just help enough other people get what they want."

Another example of when I pursued a champion connection can be seen in my partnership with business consultant Ellen Rohr. I knew about Ellen's work from magazine articles she had written, and when I had the opportunity to see her speak, I was even more impressed. At the time my company was tackling some difficult financial issues, and it was clear to me that her financial systems were what I needed. After she had finished speaking, I went to the back table where she was talking with other attendees about her various offerings, handed her my credit card, and simply said, "Give me your top package."

Eventually I not only hired Ellen to consult with my company, I also hired her to speak to my audience. Since then I have supported Ellen by letting others know about her, as well as by mentoring her as she transitioned her business from consulting to speaking and offering informational products. The result of the support I gave Ellen over the years is a strong relationship of mutual support. She teaches courses to my audience and brings new coaching members into my organization. She has become a powerful ally, colleague, and friend, and it all started by my simply handing over my credit card and essentially saying, "I believe in you."

The Second Key: Encouragement

The second key to building community in your business is encouragement. Encouragement is what inspires people to do the things they don't feel like doing, the things they fear doing, and the things they don't know they can do. Unfortunately, encouragement is pretty hard to come by these days. With all the terrible events we see on television, read about in our newspapers, and learn about on social media, it's not surprising that so many of us feel discouraged or that it affects both our personal and professional lives. We all need encouragement. We all need hope. As Zig Ziglar said, "Encouragement is the fuel on which hope runs." And when we get that encouragement, we feel like a million bucks.

In today's world it's rare for a boss or manager to give an "Attaboy" or "Attagirl" to an employee, but *your* business can be the place where people get the emotional fuel they are starving for. The Dale Carnegie Institute has long taught that what employees want more than anything is sincere and honest appreciation. And there are many different ways of showing that appreciation and providing them with encouragement. You might, for example, bring an employee up in front of the group and give him or her a plaque or certificate for a job well done. At a conference once, I saw people almost run over one another to get a gold star they could have bought by the package for a dollar. For those who are more reserved—and likely to become embarrassed by such a public display—you can send a note of appreciation or provide a kind word in private to let them know they're doing a good job. Simply saying "thank you" and recognizing them for something they did well goes a long way in today's culture.

In fact, it's particularly important to provide some kind of recognition when a member of your team is doing something right. One of the exercises I love to do when I'm making a presentation is to show the audience a blank piece of paper with a single black dot in the middle. When I ask them what they see, they always say, "a black dot." Of course, it's a trick question. Yes, there is a black dot, but what they're ignoring is all the white space around the black dot. The white space represents what your team members do well, and the black dot represents the mistakes they make. The simple truth is that if you make it a practice to talk about the white space and build them up on a regular basis, they will be encouraged and they will perform better for you.

It is equally important, though, to provide encouragement even when a member of your team isn't doing as well as he or she could be. Several years ago, I had a team member whose sales were at the bottom of the pack. Hoping to find a way to help, I spent a day making sales calls with him and in the process discovered that he didn't have very much confidence when it came to certain products and services. And because of that, when a client asked him a difficult question, he froze. During one of the calls, though, he had to give the client directions to our office, and I noticed he didn't have any trouble doing that. So between calls I pointed out how confidently he gave directions and that sales is really just giving people directions to get what they want to get. And it worked! Just providing him the encouragement he needed took him from worst to first in sales.

Step 3: Inspire Emotional Trust

If you want to build true community in your business, it is also important that you make the effort to inspire emotional trust. Emotional trust happens when you build others up. When you encourage others, you give them emotional fuel that helps them do the things they wouldn't do on their own.

The word *encouragement* means to build the heart. Emotional trust is when someone trusts another person with his or her emotions. This is important in building relationships, and it is vital to creating true community. We often don't operate in a sense of community today because of a lack of trust.

Why do we not trust others? It may be because we have lived in an environment void of support and encouragement. Many workplaces are highly competitive to the point that there is no collaboration. This environment is driven by fear of the other person advancing over us if we collaborate. And this is a real concern in many companies. If a salesperson reveals she is working on a specific prospect, a "fellow" salesperson is likely to go after that account. In the worst cases, a manager might help the second salesperson take advantage of the other. Many corporations have become a breeding ground for a "survival of the fittest" attitude.

Building community is about building one another up. It's about celebrating success *together*. It's understanding that supporting another person and creating trust helps everyone do better.

Emotional trust happens when someone begins to share his or her true feelings and emotions with another. When you encourage your team members, they are more willing to share things with you that they normally wouldn't. And when they do that, you can help them even more. It's ironic that even though we live such public lives on social media today, we often still don't trust others with our true feelings. Of course, many people have been hurt (intentionally or otherwise) by others when they've shared their deepest feelings, and so are understandably reluctant to share deeply.

But humans were not created to live that way. We all have a deep longing to have others in our lives with whom we can share our deepest thoughts and feelings. Encouraging others, getting them to place their trust in one another, is important because the more emotional trust there is, and the deeper we are able to share, the more committed we become to one another. You can build a good business without going this deep, but if you want to build community in your business and life, and if you want to experience true community at its highest level, inspiring emotional trust is crucial.

Before you can inspire emotional trust, however, you have to find out what others care about. As John C. Maxwell, one of my mentors, pointed out in his book *Intentional Living: Choosing a Life That Matters*, there is a fairly simple way to find out what people care about—to find their "why." All you have to do is ask them three questions: What do you cry about? What do you sing about? What do you dream about? If you ask these questions of your team members, as well as of yourself, you will all be inspired to find your "why." And, as John says, "When you find your why, you'll find your way."

In order to do that, you must be willing to invest time in your team so that you are able to understand their hearts, affirm their value, and give them hope. For example, in my own company there are several young leaders whom I occasionally take on trips, take out to lunch, and do fun things with in order to have an opportunity to get to know them better—to learn their hearts. Similarly, I look for ways to affirm my team's value, such as letting them know how much their contribution matters to the team and to our clients. I also try to give them hope when they need it, to provide encouragement whenever they find themselves facing difficulties, at work as well as in their personal lives. Treating people this way is what inspires emotional trust, and once you've achieved that, you will find yourself with a loyal, engaged, and committed team that helps you serve your clients better and ultimately makes both your business and your life more profitable for everyone.

Step 4: Practice Gift Exchange

An important part of nurturing relationships is recognizing and promoting one another's strengths and talents. We all have gifts, but none of us are capable of doing everything well. We all have strengths and weaknesses. In order to succeed we have to develop relationships with people, both inside and outside of the organization, who will share their abilities with us and with whom we can share ours.

Recognizing others' gifts and even promoting their gifts benefits everyone involved and, even more important, helps build a stronger bond among all those in the organization. Usually, team members view their own job as the most important job. They don't realize the importance of other roles, and they don't always appreciate the gifts others have.

For example, while I have certain gifts when it comes to business, in the early days managing money was not one of them. However, I had a partner named Scott Zack who was brilliant when it came to money. I have to admit I did not recognize his gift at the time. In fact, I always felt he was holding me back, partly because he always seemed to be complaining about the money we were spending. I didn't think it was a problem because, since one of my gifts is generating more clients, I figured no matter how much money we spent, we could make it up. We didn't understand how to appreciate one another's gifts (or at least I didn't appreciate his), which resulted in us fighting about money rather than appreciating one another's strengths and working together.

Over time I got our company so far into debt that Scott felt he had no other recourse than to sever our partnership. Some time later I realized that recognizing each other's gifts made a lot more sense than fighting over them, and I asked Scott to rejoin the company as our administration director. As we have practiced gift exchange, our companies have become extremely profitable and debt free except for equipment purchases that deliver more profits through cost savings or tax deferments.

Practicing gift exchange provides several benefits to an organization. The first is that when all of your team members are operating in their gift zone, there's a tremendous amount of energy and excitement, because everyone is essentially doing what he or she was born to do. The second is that your clients, patients, members, or guests get a phenomenal service experience because you've leveraged the gifts of every team member. The third benefit, not surprisingly, is increased profits. When everyone is operating in his or her gift zone, work is easier, there's less waste, and the team becomes effective and efficient.

As with the other steps, gift exchange is practiced outside the company as well. We must leverage the minds of others who have gifts that our team does not have. Ellen Rohr is a great example of that. We did not have the financial systems, mindset, or experience that Ellen had, and she came along during the period when Scott was not there. Once Scott returned, the power of Ellen's and Scott's gifts combined shot our profits through the roof.

The Third Key: Accountability

The third and final key is accountability. According to the Merriam-Webster dictionary, the word *accountable* means "subject to giving an account: answerable." In other words, it means being willing to accept responsibility for one's own actions. Unfortunately, in today's culture it seems that many people are unwilling to take responsibility for the results of their actions. Somehow, whenever anything goes wrong, it's always someone else's fault. Whether it's corporate fraud, government scandals, or simply blaming someone else, it seems that people think they should be able to do whatever they want, and whenever and however they want to do it, regardless of how it affects others.

What I mean by accountable is much more than the dictionary definition. In my mind accountability is key to becoming the person you were created to be. That's because it is only by being accountable that you can discover and develop your gifts and help others discover and develop theirs.

Since becoming the person you were created to be is the ultimate definition of success, it is only by being accountable that you can achieve it. In practical terms, being accountable means being true to your own values—to what you believe is important in life. And if you want to build true community in your organization, you have to determine the values that will guide that community and make sure that every member of your team, every individual in the community, operates by those values. It is only when the members of your team are accountable in this way that they, and the company, will be in a position to achieve their personal destiny.

As is the case with the first two keys, support and encouragement, as an owner or manager it is essential that you create an atmosphere of accountability, which means you have to take the first step by being accountable toward others. In order to do that, you have to live a life of accountability yourself. You have to take responsibility for your own actions, be respectful to your team members, be open to them, and allow yourself to be vulnerable. You also have to be willing to admit when you're wrong, confess that you don't have all the answers, and ask your team for feedback on how you're doing as a leader.

The idea of living this way may seem overwhelming, but I know from my own experience that it's only by doing so that you will be able to develop true community in your organization. Once you are living an accountable life, both personally and professionally—and the two *are* connected—you will be able to promote that value in your organization. And the way to do that is to take the next two steps in the process—invite openhearted encounters and build Growth PODS.

Step 5: Invite Openhearted Encounters

In taking the first steps to build community in your organization you will have developed trusting relationships with the people on your team, and it will be easier for you to share your heart with them. It is important, though, to make a point of inviting what I call open-hearted encounters by making it clear to faithful friends on your team that they can speak openly and honestly to you even if what they have to say might be hurtful.

For example, some time ago I had a manager whose performance was decidedly subpar, but I put up with it because I knew that his role was so important, that letting him go would require us to restructure the company. However, seeing what was going on and caring so much about the community, my protégé Santiago challenged me by pointing out my unwillingness to deal with the situation. I knew in my heart that letting the manager go was the right thing to do—in fact, one of my consultants had told me I should do it—but I was afraid to take action. In a different, unaccountable environment, someone might have come to me about the poor performance of the manager, but it might have been someone who was trying to advance himself rather than someone who was acting out of love for the community.

In order to experience accountability outside of your organization, you need to have coaches and mentors who will help you become the person you were created to be by helping you see the truth. Accountability builds your character, and your character is who you truly are.

Inviting openhearted encounters from your mentors is also important. For example, in 1997 I realized I needed some assistance in setting up systems in my business and invited two of my colleagues to come in as partners. Everything seemed to be going well until, less than a year later, I decided to start another business. The new business, Phenomenal Products, required me to be on the road constantly, which understandably frustrated my partners. As long as we were working together it was like magic. I was the marketing and sales person who knew how to bring in the business. Dennis was the operations person who knew how to get the work done. And Scott was the financial person who made sure our accounts were in order.

I could see that our partnership was becoming strained, and in hopes that my mentor Dr. Ralph Neighbour Jr. would be able to help, I went to talk with him. I shared with him how my partners didn't understand me and how much conflict we had, and he listened carefully for a full hour.

When I finally finished pouring out my woes, he looked at me and said, "Howard, I'm afraid you're suffering from the fear of rejection." Rejection? Me? I couldn't believe it—I thought I was the most confident person I knew. Then he went on. "You aren't willing to face the fact that it isn't working. You're making excuses because you're afraid they'll leave and you will have to give up your other business." And I realized he was right.

Of course, it should have been obvious to me, but when you're in an emotional situation, especially if fear is involved, you don't always see things as they are. This openhearted encounter with Ralph was both unexpected and transformational. It made me face reality. It also taught me a lesson that enabled me to avoid making the same kind of mistake again.

After this openhearted encounter with my mentor, I began to communicate more openly and frankly with my partners. Although it was a little too late to save the partnership, my approach saved the relationship. I bought them out, and the business became very successful. Both of them went on to do meaningful work, and one of them ended up coming back and is one of my most valued directors today.

Once you begin to live a lifestyle of accountability, you can invite your team members into these kinds of openhearted encounters. Sometimes they happen unexpectedly. They can happen intentionally, or unintentionally as a result of following the first four steps. When I value true community, pursue champion connections, inspire emotional trust, and practice gift exchange, I've set myself up to invite openhearted encounters.

This was the case one afternoon as Daena, one of my team members, was taking me to the airport. I had realized that although she was only 18 years old at the time, Daena had many gifts. The trust I built with her in a short time created an openhearted encounter that changed both of us.

On the way to the airport that day, Daena shared deeply about her fears and emotional past, which had been difficult for her. I was so moved that I purposed myself to encourage her every single day from that point on so she could gain the confidence she needed to become the person she was destined to be. It wasn't easy—community never is—but she now knows what her purpose is, and her gifts are shining more brightly today than ever before. This experience also changed me, as I discovered how much change can happen in a person in such a short amount of time.

Encounters like this don't, of course, happen with just anyone—only with those who have become faithful friends. And you obviously won't have this kind of relationship with every person on your team, but it's very powerful when the relationship does reach this level.

As you build community in your organization by supporting and encouraging others and getting involved in their lives, faithful friends will emerge. You will inspire their lives, and they will inspire yours. You can increase the likelihood of these encounters when you intentionally seek out friends who have the same values as you, both inside and outside your organization. I have many friends and associates who have no formal role in my company, and I don't have any formal role in their professional world, but we collaborate for the simple but important reason that it helps us all grow personally and professionally.

Step 6: Build Growth PODS

The sixth and final step in building community involves developing small groups, or what I call PODS—Power of Discovery Systems— that not only help move individuals toward true accountability but also help spread community throughout the organization.

A POD is a small group that meets on a regular basis for the purpose of fostering more effective communication, accountability, and implementation. Unlike what happens in a traditional meeting, in which one person speaks to the group, in a POD meeting, interaction is encouraged. These purpose-minded life support groups can be used for almost any reason—to reach company goals, keep a project moving forward, achieve personal goals, change habits, or develop members' skills or gifts.

Typically including seven to nine individuals, PODS are designed to allow participants to "discover" what they need to do rather than be taught (or worse, *told*). This is particularly important in today's society because people tend to bristle when you tell them what to do, and PODS enable them to discover important concepts on their own. When people discover something themselves, they feel a sense of ownership, which makes it more likely that they will implement it. And when they do, it is with a sense of purpose.

There is a considerable amount of precedent for forming groups like these. In the eighteenth century, Benjamin Franklin founded a group called a Junto that served the purpose, among others, of helping its members learn from one another. The original Junto spawned several other groups, and some still exist today. A contemporary of Franklin's, evangelist John Wesley, established what he called class meetings, where participants shared deeply and openly in small groups. Wesley's influence sparked a revival in England, and his work led to the founding of the Methodist Church.

Jeff Sutherland, in his book *Scrum: The Art of Doing Twice the Work in Half the Time*, outlines how small groups using a new methodology for project development can outproduce other types of teams. And leadership expert John C. Maxwell, in collaboration with Jerry Anderson, is using a small group system called RoundTables that is transforming values in South America.

Jerry Wiles, regional director of North America for The International Orality Network, is leading a movement in worldwide missions using a method called Orality that utilizes a combination of small groups, storytelling, and a specific method for implementation and duplication. This looks very promising as a leadership method.

These groups can also be called cell groups or life groups that meet on a regular basis to learn and grow together. The functioning of cell groups in an organization is similar to how a living organism is made up of cells that grow and multiply, therefore creating life.

Growth PODS bring all three keys, support, encouragement, and accountability, and the previous five steps into one simple structure that will not only help your company be more productive but, more important, help your team build community. PODS are the building blocks for expanding a sense of belonging, then a sense of community, and eventually, the ultimate goal of true community.

A true, genuine community is one in which all those who are part of it are committed to one another in every way possible, whether it's a family, an organization, or, for that matter, an entire society. And as you've now seen, support, encouragement, and accountability are the three keys that are necessary to create true community. It is important to understand, though, that no matter how much you want it to happen, community is not something you can force. You cannot make people change. It will be difficult in the beginning as both you and your team members struggle to shed counterproductive values and habits.

A true, genuine community is one in which all those who are part of it are committed to one another in every way possible.

However, armed with the knowledge that, deep down, all human beings have a longing for belonging, and keeping in mind that you and your team will create the vision and values that will energize your community, you can develop the kind of environment that facilitates a greater level of trust, a deeper level of sharing, and the kind of accountability that will enable true community to thrive in your organization.

In the next few chapters, you'll learn the Six Steps to Building Community at a deeper level, and then you'll learn how to systematize your organization so you can intentionally create a community brand experience.

Once you've successfully accomplished all of this, you'll be poised to reap the benefits:

An inspired, engaged team

Happy, devoted clients, and

Bigger, healthier profits

STEP 1: VALUE TRUE COMMUNITY

Many years ago, I didn't have the best culture in the first small business I started. When I arrived at the office, the only thing on my mind was what hadn't been done yet and what needed to get done. My small team and I valued our clients at the highest level, and we provided our clients with the most outstanding service experience ever and outshined our competition by a mile.

When I first started the company, we worked unbelievable hours, from early in the morning until late at night, and we had a strong community. But as the business grew, I brought on partners and we began hiring more people. We grew very fast, and in the midst of that growth, I started my training company, which meant I was traveling constantly doing seminars and coaching clients. I left a leadership vacuum behind. We didn't have the support, encouragement, and accountability in place. We no longer had community. We had a collection of people.

We began working on systems, and we had a strong mission, but our team was engaged only to the point necessary to get the job done, and some of our team members were disengaged. A review of my journal during that time read:

> My absence over the past two years has created a great division in the ranks. It seems everyone complains about everyone else . . . I must schedule a staff meeting to begin mentoring community.

Over time, we became a community again. What changed? For starters, leadership changed. I built the leadership team by supporting them, encouraging them, and helping them be accountable to the vision they had of themselves. They did the same for me. We established a vision for who we wanted to become and our core values. Over time, as I learned more about community, our whole culture changed to one that could be described as supportive, encouraging, and accountable. Today it is a loving atmosphere, and highly effective and profitable as well. Without overworking the staff, I might add.

We began to value one another and one another's role. The first of the Six Steps to Building Community is to value true community. We cannot build something we do not value. Valuing true community is assessing your vital need for deep, trusting relationships with people of shared beliefs to help one another become all you can be.

Now, I'll turn this on to you and ask whether you truly value community at the level you need to lead your team into a sense of community. As leaders, we all must examine what we truly value. And we can find out what we value very easily simply by watching our actions. For example, if I say I value health but I eat a quart of ice cream every night, what do I really value? Ice cream!

As I mentioned in the previous chapter, when we value something at a high level, we tend to protect it and promote it. When you value something, you protect it so that you don't lose it. You care for it so that it doesn't diminish in value. When you value something, you promote it. You talk about it. You proudly display it for all to see.

Your team members can be your greatest asset or your biggest liability, and that depends on your skill as a leader. My goal for this book is to coach you from where you are now as a leader to the ultimate goal of building true community in your business.

Your team members can be your greatest asset or your biggest liability, and that depends on your skill as a leader.

Although you may be a long way from that now, it's not only possible to achieve true community, but very likely if you follow the Six Steps to Building Community. You may be starting out with a terrible culture right now. You will not develop a sense of community in your organization without being intentional about it. In order to be highly intentional, you must place a high value on community and its benefits to you, your team, and your clients, patients, members, guests, or donors. If you don't value genuine community yourself, you won't model it well, and your team won't buy into the idea. As you begin the process, it is helpful to assess your commitment to this process.

One major reason that we must check our values as they relate to building community is that it won't be an easy climb. Human beings are creatures of habit and routine, and everyone is selfish and territorial to a certain degree. All of us have fears, and one of the biggest fears we all have is the fear of being vulnerable. We've all been taken advantage of, and your team members won't immediately trust you when you decide to change. It will take time and effort on everyone's part.

The good news is that by climbing these steps, you'll have a shot at developing deep relationships among your team members. Even at the early stages of building community, your culture will improve and you'll reap many benefits.

Building a sense of community starts with simply valuing your team members. When you value people, you'll care about them, and you'll support them. Support includes helping your team members win at work and win at home. My three decades of owning a business and two decades of training small business owners has revealed that helping team members reach their personal goals is one of the most powerful things you can do, because when you help them, they will want to help you reach your goals.

The Human Bridge

Valuing true community is the first step under the support key. Supporting others is being the "human bridge" that helps others have the life they want to have. When you help others with their lives, they'll want to help you. When you give to others, they will give back. If you consistently find that you help others and they don't support you, perhaps you have attracted the wrong people. But don't blame them. Whoever hired such a person is the one who needs to be coached. In other words, if you are consistently hiring people who do not support the vision of the company, you have a hiring problem. It would be wise to review how you are attracting candidates and why you are attracting people who don't go the extra mile for you or others.

You can begin the process of supporting others by simply asking those on your team about their personal goals and dreams. It might be to buy a house, run a marathon, or learn a skill. You can then begin to help them in those endeavors. For example, if someone wanted to buy a home, do you know people who could help him with that? You could give him information or connect him with other people. If you see an article or blog post about someone who ran her first marathon or you saw some information about the skill a person wanted to learn, you could simply help her with information or connections. Although this is a simple gesture, my experience has been that many business owners or managers don't know what their team members' personal goals are.

You might also call this the Law of Reciprocity, which in essence says, "If you help me, I'll help you." Once again, my friend John Maxwell, who has been recognized as the number one leadership expert in the world by *Inc.* magazine, says, "Leadership is influence. Nothing more, nothing less. You gain influence in someone else's life by adding value to them."

President Dwight Eisenhower proclaimed, "Leadership [is] the art of getting someone else to do something that you want done because he wants to do it." Why would the person want to do it? Because you've added value to him or her. You've helped the person get what he or she wants. Not just at work but at home.

If you don't adopt this value of helping other people, the rest of this book won't be much use to you. The first step, value true community, is the foundation for everything else. How do you value relationships? How do you value others? How do you value shared beliefs, shared values, and shared goals?

Recently, I was holding a two-day POD Experience for a group of clients in Philadelphia, and one of the members had been struggling with connecting with his employees. Like most business owners and managers, he just assumed that people should automatically have the same values he does, including the same work ethic.

Another client moaned that certain things are just "common sense." Although that may be true, the fact is that everyone isn't going to think like you or see things the way you do. If they did, they would probably have your job. That doesn't mean that you look down on others or that they are less important; it just means that you must see things as they see them in order to help them. And you won't do that unless you value them.

Valuing others means caring for others. Do you really and truly care about people? Many years ago, an associate of mine began to provide technical training as a consultant. He confessed to me that he didn't really care about people, but he knew he had a lot of technical knowledge that he could charge people for. I probably don't have to tell you that he was not successful. In fact, he has struggled with just about every job and every venture he has gotten involved in since that time.

The owner of a very successful small business told me once, "I used to hate my employees, but now I love them." He told me that he would come into the office after his employees had gone into the field, and he would leave the office before they got back so that he didn't have to "deal" with them. This is obviously the opposite of building community.

I was curious how the transition from hating his employees to loving them had taken place, so I asked him some questions about it. I identified four significant steps he took:

He Took Personal Responsibility

He realized that the problems in his company had more to do with him than with his team. One of the greatest lessons a leader can learn is that it isn't them; it's you. And if it is them, who hired them? If you did, guess who it comes back to? You!

Maybe you're like one of my clients who just became president of a company and inherited a team that's not so great. On a coaching call, he told me about a horrific staff meeting at which the employees attacked one another verbally to the point that everyone stormed out of the meeting.

The good news is that this client has already been through the process of building community with his own company. The better news is that he has a vision and values for his new post and new team. Whether the existing team stays intact or not, he'll be successful if he sticks with the proven process.

Another friend of mine was a green consultant just out of college, and he took on a client that had a culture so bad that when a disagreement took place in the first team meeting, two of the team members literally got into a fistfight. The good news is that he helped that company build community, and it became world famous and has an amazing culture today. The consultant helped the team members open a constructive dialogue rather than fighting against each other. During one of their monthly dinner meetings, one of the employees came up with an idea about how to treat their customers that no one liked at first. But because they now had a culture of hearing one another out, they decided to try it out.

He Became Grateful for His Team

Next, the business owner began to realize that without his team, he would not be able to have the success he wanted for his business. Although this seems obvious, isn't it true that we all sometimes take relationships for granted?

When you truly value something, you cherish it. He began to cherish his team members. Unfortunately, some leaders have to lose a good person to realize what they had.

He Began to Get to Know Them

He started taking interest in his team members' lives. What were their goals? What were their interests? What dreams did they have? What was their story? He began to learn about their aspirations and their difficulties.

The television show *Undercover Boss* sends CEOs into the front lines of their organizations incognito. There, the CEO finds out what's really going on in the company and most often finds people who have endured great difficulties in their personal lives and are doing a phenomenal job at work despite the difficulties.

The CEO does what the direct supervisor should have been doing all along. Of course the direct supervisor isn't doing it because he or she was never trained to do so. The climax of each episode is a tear-jerking feeling of support and encouragement.

What if that feeling had been fostered from the top from the beginning? What would your company be like if you approached your business every day like the ending of *Undercover Boss*?

Author Bob Burg often remarks, "People do business with those they know, like, and trust." This is not only true for customers but is also true of team members. Dale Carnegie said, "People support a world they help create." Get to know your team members by spending time with them. Take them out to lunch. Accept invitations to their family events if you're privileged to be invited.

He Became Intentional About Supporting His Team Members

He began to support them in their personal lives. Not only did it help him feel differently about his employees, his support caused his team members to engage and to be more productive and effective. And of course that leads to happier customers and bigger profits.

Therefore, the first step includes going the "extra mile" to help your team members achieve their personal and professional goals through mentoring, coaching, and teaching. When employees feel that management cares about them—that the company is interested in them as human beings—they tend to be not only more engaged but even inspired to help the company reach its goals.

A Leader Is a Coach

Community begins with coaching. When you value someone, you spend time with the person getting to know him or her. Instead of seeing yourself as a boss or manager, start viewing yourself as a coach. The origin of the word coach is *carriage*, which is simply a vehicle to help people get from where they are to where they want or need to be.

Community begins with coaching.

A boss is just someone who tells others what to do. The employees may do what you say, but they may be disgruntled as they do it. And they could very well be disengaged behind the scenes and actually working against you. Obviously, people need to do their job, but as Dale Carnegie points out in his classic book *How to Win Friends and Influence People*, you'll be more successful attracting people to your ideas with honey than you will with vinegar. It is much more effective to be a coach than it is to be a boss.

Care and Coach vs. Command and Control

Many business owners still use the "command and control" style of management, which entails the taskmaster simply barking out orders while everyone cowers down to his or her command. Unfortunately, this style of management doesn't work. People are not engaged—there is no loyalty, no care, and no joy in the workplace.

Of course the work has to be done. And it does get done in the "command and control" environment, but it is not done well, and when the taskmaster isn't watching, the employee will tend to slack off. In contrast, leaders who have paid attention to the trends today will understand that impactful leadership is about "care and coach" rather than command and control. When leaders show they care about their team members, the members will work harder for that leader.

When you truly care about others, you'll coach them to success.

Impactful leadership is about "care and coach"
rather than command and control.

At these companies, leaders see being a coach as an important part of their role. The most impactful coaches do the following:

- A coach gets people from where they are to where they need to be.

- A coach inspires people to reach their peak potential.

- A coach holds people accountable.

- A coach ensures people have received training.

- A coach makes sure people are in the right position.

- A coach exercises authority while remaining responsible for developing team members.

A good coach knows what his or her players' gifts, strengths, and weaknesses are. He or she is in tune with the personal habits that affect players' performance. In order to know these things, a coach has to spend time with the players.

A good coach can see a player's potential even when the player can't. A coach holds the players accountable. Not doing so affects the players' future potential. Later in this book, we will cover accountability in greater detail.

A good coach makes sure each player has received appropriate training. My colleague Ellen Rohr says, "Tracking without training is mean." So many times leaders assume that certain things come naturally to others. It would be ridiculous to track a player's batting average and hold it against him or her if the player had never been properly trained on hitting the ball, yet that's what happens in business all the time. Once you train someone, be sure to track performance so you can help him or her improve.

In the classic business book *Good to Great*, author Jim Collins shares that great companies "get the right people on the bus." Then they get them in the right seat. As you get to know your team members' personality profiles and their gifts, talents, and interests, you can make sure you get them in the right position. That's the coach's responsibility.

As a leader, you not only have authority, you have a responsibility to develop your team. How you use your authority will make the difference in your effectiveness as a leader. Leaders who use their authority to boost their own ego or advance their personal agenda will reap a disengaged—and perhaps *actively* disengaged—team, and going to work every day will not be enjoyable or meaningful for anyone.

A Leader Is Not a Manager

A manager is someone who accounts for resources, organizes processes, and reports data to directors. Although these things are very important, they won't matter much if the manager doesn't have the willing cooperation of the team members. Leaders develop people.

Of course, at the same time, as a leader, you must avoid creating a sense of entitlement. Supporting someone is not doing everything *for*

him or her or providing everything for him or her. Supporting someone personally is helping him or her with information, physical help,
contacts, or resources. If people are not doing their part, a coaching
session is in order to talk about their role in helping themselves.

Supporting people means ensuring that they have the tools and
the training they need to be successful. It doesn't mean that you enable their weaknesses or dysfunction. A community environment is
a highly accountable environment, but it is practiced with care and
concern for the person rather than the harsh treatment employees
may endure in some workplaces today.

Be a Leader Mate

In 2011, my family and I travelled to Australia with Tom Ziglar and
his daughter Alexandra. My nickname for Tom was "boss," and he
called me by that nickname as well. Of course, people in Australia call
one another "mate," so Tom and I began calling one another "boss
mate" on that trip. As we began to think about the difference between
a boss and a leader, we changed it to "leader mate."

A mate helps you. A mate is there for you when you need him
or her. Everyone in the company is a leader because everyone has influence in one another's life. So be a leader mate to others, instead of
a boss.

My experience tells me that when you hire the right people, show
interest in them, and intentionally help them reach their goals personally and professionally, most often they will want to help you
reach your goals as well.

Alcoholics Anonymous involves a strong sense of community,
and each individual has a sponsor—someone to support him or her.
In fact, AA was started by two men who simply began by supporting
each other.

You can begin *your* journey of building a phenomenal community experience in your company by simply finding someone in your company to support. Find a mate. Be a mate. And you'll also want to support key people outside your organization, as we will see in the next chapter.

STEP 2: PURSUE CHAMPION CONNECTIONS

Our working definition of leadership is "Leadership is effectively communicating your vision." Patrick Lencioni teaches us in *The Advantage* that the first discipline in organizational health is to build a cohesive leadership team.

> Patrick Lencioni teaches us in *The Advantage*
> that the first discipline in organizational health is
> to build a cohesive leadership team.

Pursuing champion connections means investing intentionally in relationships that have the potential to become strong alliances of support and mission. On the inside of your organization, you'll want to begin by selecting a couple of people on your leadership team who you know are loyal to you. Begin intentionally investing in those relationships, and then you can expand the size of the group from there.

For example, in my company, the way we began to transform our culture from rigid and internally unkind (even though we were doing great work for our clients) was through a powerful champion connection with a young leader on my team. Santiago wanted to win. Along with the rest of the team, he was frustrated with the lackluster performance of the company. He could see what I saw—that our company could be a *great* company.

I selected Santiago, my former partner Scott, and another young leader as my core leadership team to turn the company around. And turn it around they did. The company went from unprofitable to extremely profitable, and over time a strong sense of community and pride developed. Today, the company is like a happy, functional family. We have true community.

When I do conferences in Houston, we invite the small business owner attendees to take a tour of our company. I recently had a half-day coaching session with a couple that had been on the tour, and as they were about to leave the meeting room, the man turned around to shake my hand and looked me in the eye. "Let me tell you something," he started. "I was on your company tour yesterday, and all of your people had a glow about them. I'm very impressed. You walk the talk." Of course, that made me proud, but it also confirmed that my leadership team is doing a great job of building community at the company even when I'm not there. When leadership supports, encourages, and properly holds team members accountable, the result is an engaged team that is obvious to even a visitor.

In order to win in business, we must pursue champion connections. Find one or two people who you know "have your back." Find one or two you know you can count on and build a core leadership team. In *The Heart of Change: Real-Life Stories of How People Change*

Their Organizations, John Kotter outlines eight steps to create massive change. The first one is to create a sense of urgency. Understanding the great need to create community in your company and the associated benefits (inspired team members, loyal customers, and healthy profits) should create a sense of urgency among you and your team members. Kotter's second step is to build a guiding team.

In order to build a guiding team, you'll want to create your first Growth POD. Your first POD is your Leadership POD, where you can build community with your core leadership team. Once that group is established, you'll be able to create PODS throughout your company. In order to do this effectively, you'll want to understand the rest of this book, and you'll want to become skilled in facilitating a POD.

For now, pursue champion connections inside your company and intentionally invest in those relationships. Find out what these leaders' personal and professional goals are. Find out what their personal values are. Share your vision with them and get input from them.

Your first small group will become the heartbeat of the company. This is where you'll flesh out the vision for your company. This is where you'll talk about what really matters in the company. You'll develop your mission, values, and purpose together. This is where you'll learn how to create community together and you'll "do life together." You'll support one another, encourage one another, and be accountable to one another. A Growth POD is not an exclusive internal group but a cell that is expected to multiply.

Your first small group will become the
heartbeat of the company.

Look for Outside Connections, Too

We need to pursue champion connections not only inside the company but outside the company as well. We not only need an internal community, we need to develop community outside the company to gain the support we need ourselves as leaders. As a business owner or leader, you need support, encouragement, and accountability. Outside the company, we need to intentionally invest in relationships that have the potential of becoming strong alliances of support and mission.

As I mentioned earlier, Tom Ziglar is a great example for me. I pursued a relationship with Ziglar but had no idea what would become of the connection. The result is that we've been able to impact people around the world because of our relationship. The challenge is that you don't know which relationships will blossom and which ones won't. Both inside and outside your company, as the leader, you must continually plant, water, and nurture the seeds of relationships. Some will sprout and grow, and others (even though you may feel strongly about them) simply won't. That's just the nature of building strategic alliances.

I often share with members of my coaching community that the most important skill they can develop is the skill of building relationships. All of business and all of life is about relationships. Whether you're building relationships with those inside or outside your company, it all starts with support. It simply starts by serving others.

Pursuing champion connections is about finding a win-win-win scenario. Yes, there are three wins here—you help your connection win, his or her customer wins, and you win. How do we help others win? How do our mutual clients win? And how do we win? All three parties need to win. I never asked Tom Ziglar to be the exclusive small business coach for Ziglar. In fact, I never asked for anything. I just served him and his company.

We had lunch from time to time when I was in Dallas. Later on, I invited Tom and Julie (Zig's daughter) to speak at my conference. I simply served and supported them. Because of my support, they asked me to do some video webcasts for them to teach their audience how to build a business. As the relationship grew, I encouraged them. Today we're business partners because of that. Now, as partners, we have a high level of accountability, and the Ziglar family is part of my community. After leaving Ziglar one day I posted on my social media "I always feel like family when I'm at Ziglar"—to which Julie replied "You *ARE* family, Howard!"

Gary Keller, co-founder of Keller Williams Realty, the largest residential real estate company in the United States, writes in his book *The One Thing: The Surprisingly Simple Truth Behind Extraordinary Results*, "No one succeeds alone." In fact, Gary's journey to the top began with a coaching session where he realized he needed to step down as CEO and focus on finding and developing his core leadership team. He needed 14 people. Installing that team put Keller Williams on an unprecedented growth path of 40 percent year over year growth for over a decade.

"No one succeeds alone."

—GARY KELLER

Attracting a Strong Community

Building community inside and outside your company creates a powerful combination that will inspire you and your team to greater heights in your business. You'll see how powerful it can be for your clients in a later chapter as we discuss how to build a community brand experience.

Building meaningful relationships is what matters most in life. At the end of our lives, the only thing we will have left is our legacy. And building meaningful relationships creates a legacy. Of course the company needs to make money, and it is more likely that it will when you build community inside and outside the company.

Your best clients, team members, vendors, and associates will most likely come from your intentional relationship-building activities. Building your network will have a dramatic impact on your life and business.

The digital revolution has seduced us into thinking that connecting on social media is just as good as meeting in person, but it's not. Remember that virtual community is an oxymoron. Connecting with people in person and building real relationships is the key.

My experience has taught me that building a strong network of relationships has brought me the best team members as well. Here's a simple process I've used to attract phenomenal team members:

Identify People Who Have the Same Values You Do

In other words, you have the same worldview, you have the same outlook on life. Diversity of gifts is important, but having similar values helps build a strong community. Kenny Pelletier and I attended the same church. I knew Kenny would be a good addition to our inside sales team because he was a disc jockey at a Christian radio station, which meant he could follow a script. We generate a lot of phone calls with our marketing, and our inside sales positions don't require a high level of experience, just the ability to follow a script and get callers the information they need.

Kenny was in the Tuesday night small group where I first discovered community. And his daughter Elise was the one baby-sitting my son in the other room. Little did I know that Elise would also come to work at my company and marry a young man by the name of

Santiago who would head up the transformation of my company—and become like a son to me.

Identify People Who Have Different Gifts Than You

I'll get into this when we talk about team building later on, but I want to give you some insight into the process right now while we're talking about pursuing champion connections.

Rick Jones was with the Dale Carnegie Institute for 33 years. He owned the Houston franchise for over 20 years, winning the highest award available 5 out of 10 years. My wife (who was in sales) called on Rick, and we became friends. I supported Rick in every way that I could, and I asked him to speak at my conferences from time to time.

About three years after Rick sold his franchise, I called him for a "catch-up lunch." Intentionally pursuing championship connections means staying in touch with people to see what's happening in their life and to support and encourage them.

"I'm thinking about going into coaching," Rick confessed over lunch. "My noncompete agreement is over now, and I want to spend the rest of my life doing something to really make a difference in other people's lives."

At the time, I had just become the small business coach for Ziglar, and I knew I was going to need someone like Rick for our Ziglar clients. As I shared what I was doing with Ziglar, his interest grew.

Rick has been on my team as a coach for six years now and has helped many people in our community literally change their lives, but he has also become like a father to me, and he loves me like a son. That's community.

Michelle has the gift of logistics. She's perfect for operations. She gets me around the world without a hitch, runs all of my events—which include four major conferences each year and a multitude of workshops and speeches—while handling all of our membership accounts. Without even looking at the massive files, she can tell you exactly what a member's status is. She's been with me for almost 10 years, and she's like a mom to us all.

Victoria is gifted in the area of digital marketing. With a marketing degree in hand, she interviewed in the corporate world only to find out how ugly the culture was behind the curtain. She has served for five years as my marketing manager, and she's like a daughter to us.

Johann also has the gift of operations. He runs the operations for one of my companies that does several million per year, and he's only 32 years old. He started with me when he was 19. He is also like a son to me.

Scott has the gift of finance. He's a wizard when it comes to money, and he handles all of my financial affairs, but more important, he is like a brother to me. Formerly partners, we've been through the ups and downs of business and of life together.

In every one of these relationships, I've served these team members in one way or another that created a sense of belonging, that moved to a sense of community and to a place now where we *are* a community. Any of these team members would get up in the middle of the night for one another for any reason. My team takes care of my home, my finances, and my personal affairs not because they have to but because they want to.

As you can see, I've used the terms *father*, *son*, *daughter*, and *brother*. They were not family members when they were hired, but they became like family. A community is like a family.

Identify Future Candidates

When marketing your company, you don't wait until you need a customer to start marketing. In much the same way, you don't wait until you need a team member to build a relationship with him or her. Always keep your eyes out for future talent. Aliki is the daughter of a couple we've been friends with for over 30 years. I could see Aliki's gifts early on. I've known her all her life, and she has always been quick and smart, and she has a gift of connecting with others. Much like my wife, Denise, she has never met a stranger and immediately makes a connection.

I've learned to add value to people like Aliki even when they're children. For one thing, they need the encouragement that's in short supply today, but also, if you're the one who gives them the one thing they long for—the one thing all humans want, which is love, acceptance, and validation—you'll be the one they think of when it's time to apply for a job.

Of course you don't do that just because you hope someday in years to come a person *might* come to work for you. You do it because it's the right thing to do. You do it because you *value* other people. You *value* community.

When Aliki was 21, she came to work as a part-time marketing rep while she was going to college. Upon finishing college, she was determined to climb the proverbial corporate ladder. I knew it wouldn't be the right fit for someone like Aliki—someone who has good values. But she had to try it, and she got some big promises from the company that recruited her.

Over the six months that she worked for that company, I checked in with her on a regular basis to "see how it's going." The first few months were good, but after six months of becoming disgusted by the backstabbing, negative atmosphere, she was ready to come back "home." She had a degree in entrepreneurship, and I offered her the position of marketing manager in one of my companies.

Aliki tripled our partner referrals in less than a year and was promoted to marketing director of that company. During a convention in Las Vegas we were having lunch as a team, and Aliki became very emotional as she shared how much she loves our team. "You guys are like my family," she gushed with tears.

In 2011, my wife and I went to Australia with Tom Ziglar and his daughter Alexandra. She was only 17 at the time, and instead of discounting her as the "kid" on the trip, I took interest in her goals and dreams and I treated her well. I made her feel comfortable and treated her like an adult during the seminars Tom and I were doing. Over the next five years as I interacted with Ziglar, I purposed myself to treat her like my own daughter. My acknowledging birthdays, accomplishments, and just encouraging her caused her to see me as more than just one of her dad's buddies. Upon graduating from the University of Oklahoma with honors, out of all the companies she could have chosen, she elected to join our team. At only 22 years old, the intelligence, poise, grace, and creativity Alexandra has will ensure she becomes a superstar in our organization.

The manager of our warehouse has a young son whom he brings to work from time to time. Over the years, as I was building that company, I purposed myself to always have something for Gabriel when he showed up. I made sure Denise kept me stocked with a variety of toys so that if any child of an employee or client happened to be in the office, I would give them a toy or buy them a soda. Gabriel was certain to stop by my office when he was there! Now that he's a teenager, I usually give him cash when I see him, but the point is, I want him to know there is someone who cares about him. I want him to have hope that there are people in this world who care about him. Will he come to work for us? I don't know, but the chances are that he will, and if not, he will always support what his daddy does for a living. Growing a phenomenal business is about engaging the entire community.

The idea here is not to promote nepotism but to highlight the fact that all of business is about relationships. Michelle, my operations manager at my coaching company, is a mom with five children. Although I did not know her when she was hired, she became like the company "mom." Obviously, new hires have to have a minimum level of experience or knowledge unless they go into an entry-level position. In that case, they can be trained in the skills they need for their position.

While we're talking about young people, allow me make a special note about millennials. There's a lot of talk about millennials being lazy, distracted with texting or social media. Buying into a blanket statement like that isn't a good idea, because the fact is that 50-year-olds can also be lazy and distracted. The way I prefer to see it is that young people are connected. They know technology, and they have lots of energy and creativity. That is, if you choose the right ones. As you can see, I've attracted some phenomenal young people, so it doesn't have anything to do with age. It has everything to do with values. If you attract people with the right values and you lead them well, young people can revolutionize your business and older people can bring wisdom to it. The most important function as a leader is to hire the right person with the right kind of values and gifts for your community.

Young people are starving for real relationships just like everyone else. Maybe more so, since they've lived most of their lives with online, superficial relationships. The *Wall Street Journal* recently reported that child suicides have doubled in the last decade. The biggest group? Teenage girls. One can only imagine the stress they must feel to fit the image of the idealized woman they see on their screens. The report states that the causes are inconclusive, but researchers suspect cyber-bullying.

In their book *Beauty Begins: Making Peace with Your Reflection*, mother and daughter team Chris Shook and Megan Shook Alpha share the difference between being beautiful and being pretty. There's a difference. Teenage girls today compare themselves to the pretty people they see on their screens. But understanding the inherent value and beauty of a human being brings joy and fulfillment that being "pretty" never can. Young girls fall into a battle of trying to appear "pretty," but deep down they don't feel pretty. When community members help one another understand that real beauty comes from the inside, the self-image of that young person changes and helps her become a happier person.

Hiring young people who can grow in your community can be a powerful force. In fact, in his book *Community: The Structure of Belonging*, Peter Block states, "Youth are a unifying force in community . . . an alternative future opens up when we shift our view of youth . . . from problem to possibility, from deficiency to gift."

In *Lost in Transition: The Dark Side of Emerging Adulthood*, Christian Smith and his collaborators draw on 230 in-depth interviews with a broad cross-section of emerging adults (ages 18 to 23) to investigate the difficulties young people face today, the underlying causes of those difficulties, and the consequences both for individuals and for American society as a whole. They have this to say:

> Teenagers and emerging adults desperately need other mature and concerned adults who genuinely care about and for them. Young people need to be loved, to put it as plainly as possible. They need to be engaged, challenged, mentored, and enjoyed. They, like every human being, need to be appropriately cared for, no matter how autonomous and self-sufficient they may think they are.

Add Value to Them (Even If They Aren't on the Team Yet)

In every case above, I and/or my team added value to the person if we knew him or her before the hire. Add value to everyone you meet, and they will be attracted to you and to your company.

Find ways to support people you want on your team. Find ways to encourage them. When you're continually investing in those you want on your team and you're investing in enough of them, you'll always have people attracted to you.

In the next chapter, we'll move from support to encouragement.

STEP 3: INSPIRE
EMOTIONAL TRUST

The second key to building community is encouragement. Encouragement is the emotional fuel people need to do the things they are afraid to do. Encouragement means to give courage. Many managers use negative comments, manipulation, and underhanded gestures to try to get others to do something they want done. This approach is discouraging, and discouragement removes courage. It literally freezes your team member with fear.

Encouragement is the emotional fuel people need to do
the things they are afraid to do.

Everyone has fears, and we all need courage to face those fears and grow out of our comfort zones. Everyone has strengths and weaknesses, and everyone lacks confidence in some area of his or her life or work. We all need someone in our life to encourage us to do the things that we may be afraid to do, whether that is taking on a new role at work, pursuing a goal, or facing a difficult situation. Phenomenal leaders care about others, and as a leader, you can reap tremendous benefits and see increased implementation as a result. When encouragement becomes part of your company culture, others will fill that role as well as team members begin to encourage one another.

Fear produces stress, harmful chemicals that are extremely taxing on the human body. An unhealthy amount of fear among team members produces an unhealthy organization. A stressed-out team member simply isn't going to be effective long term. Stress eventually takes its toll. Creating an encouraging environment creates more peace and harmony in the workplace. Your company can be the safe haven— the place where team members look forward to coming each day. The extra bonus is that people who have lower stress are healthier and are therefore present and more productive.

Fear may be a constant companion to some of your team members, and they need someone to encourage them. Getting rid of fear is not the goal. Instead try to show them they can find success by moving forward in the face of fear. That's courage. As a leader, you can be an encourager to your team, and that will inspire emotional trust, which simply means that others will trust you with their emotions. The reason that's important is that you haven't truly connected with someone until you know his or her true feelings and that he or she is buying into you and your vision.

Many people aren't naturally positive and don't naturally encourage others. Whether that is because they lack confidence themselves, they don't have the awareness of the importance of encouragement, or they're downright selfish, we tend to live in the "me" generation. In order to build community, leaders must move from *me* to *we*. Many leaders aren't confident themselves, so they revert back to "command and control" rather than care and coach.

TED Talk sensation Simon Sinek struck a chord with his book *Start with Why: How Great Leaders Inspire Everyone to Take Action* and continued to inspire those seeking to understand the depths of leadership with *Leaders Eat Last: Why Some Teams Pull Together and Others Don't.* The title of Chapter 3 is "Belonging: From Me to We."

Here's an excerpt from that chapter: "This feeling of belonging, of shared values and a deep sense of empathy, dramatically increases trust, cooperation and problem solving." Using the United States Marines as an example, he says "they operate in a strong Circle of Safety."

> "This feeling of belonging, of shared values and a deep sense of empathy, dramatically increases trust, cooperation and problem solving."
>
> **—SIMON SINEK**

He talks about the fact that the world around is filled with danger—things trying to make our lives miserable:

> Intimidation, humiliation, isolation, feeling dumb, feeling useless and rejection are all stresses we try to avoid inside the organization. But the danger inside is controllable and it should be the goal of leadership to set a culture free of danger from each other. And the way to do that is by giving people a sense of belonging . . . only when we feel we are in a Circle of Safety will we pull together as a unified team . . . the primary role of leadership is to look out for those inside their Circle.

Once you've taken the first two steps, value true community and pursue champion connections, you'll have created a fertile environment for the next step, which is to inspire emotional trust—demonstrating commitment to the individual through the investment of time, understanding people's hearts, affirming their value, and giving them hope. You inspire emotional trust by encouraging the heart.

Here's what leadership legends Kouzes and Posner had to say in their book *Encouraging the Heart*:

> Leaders create relationships, and one of these relationships is between individuals and their work. Ultimately we all work for a purpose, and that common purpose has to be served if we are to feel encouraged. Encouraging the heart only works if there's a fit between the person, the work, and the organization. . . .
>
> And the heart of leadership is caring. Without caring, leadership has no purpose. And without showing others you care and what you care about, other people won't care about what you say or what you know. As a relationship, leadership requires a connection between leaders and their constituents over matters, in the simplest sense, of the heart. . . .
>
> Encouragement is about being generous and charitable. It's about having a "big heart." When leaders encourage the heart of their constituents, they are also showing how profoundly grateful they are for the dedication and commitment others have shown to the cause.

In case you're wondering whether this idea is too "soft," consider what else they had to say:

> It's about the toughness and tenderness. Guts and grace. Firmness and fairness. Fortitude and gratitude. Passion and compassion.

> "The heart of leadership is caring."
> —JAMES M. KOUZES AND BARRY Z. POSNER,
> *Encouraging the Heart*

A positive, caring, upbeat attitude doesn't create entitled employees who become unproductive. Research clearly shows that people who feel cared for will care about the company and work harder for it. Besides that, the third key is accountability, and you'll learn a simple way to keep your team members on track with the easiest coaching process ever.

The natural progression of building community goes from support (valuing others at a high level and building a relationship with them by serving them), to encouragement (inspiring others and affirming their gifts), then to accountability (helping others become the person they want to become).

Teaching Courage
Through Encouragement

There's nothing soft about courage. Therefore, there's nothing soft about encouragement. And there's nothing soft about the cost factor of losing valuable team members because they weren't treated right or they did not have the support and encouragement required to retain them.

Consider the Leadership Challenge studies done by Jim Kouzes and Barry Posner that haven't changed in a quarter of a century: The chief reason people leave a job is limited praise and recognition.

Surveys of millions of employees reveal that feeling appreciated and feeling that they are being informed about things that are happening remain at the top of the list of things employees care about. Not the opportunity for advancement. Not pay.

We must continually remind ourselves as leaders that people want to feel loved, validated, and important and that their lives matter. We have a tremendous opportunity to create that feeling in our organizations, but we must be intentional about it.

So, How Do You Encourage People?

Here are a number of ways to encourage people.

Know Their Story

In the comedic film *What Women Want*, Mel Gibson could read women's minds by hearing their inner voices. A shy office girl who had gone unappreciated had a poor self-image and was contemplating suicide. Gibson's character was able to encourage her. You may have employees whose loved ones are struggling with cancer, or maybe they have other tremendous challenges that you don't know about. Or you may have a common interest that you're unaware of. Someone once said, "Everyone is lovable when you get to know their story."

Affirm Their Value

Every human being has inherent value, but most people suffer from a poor self-image and need someone to affirm their value. Again, every human being wants to be loved, wants to be valued, and wants to know that his or her life matters.

I mentioned Santiago earlier. He has been one of the greatest blessings in my life. He came in the form of a 17-year-old Columbian refugee, and he rose through the ranks of my companies and is now one of my top coaches. He knows my systems like no one else and can do any of my presentations. His positive, "can-do" attitude is infectious and encourages others. He encourages me because I first encouraged him.

I affirmed Santiago's value by helping him develop himself personally and professionally. Valuing his worth and investing in training for him encouraged him to step up to new levels. Great leaders make it a habit to encourage others. Encourage people to do the things they fear. Encourage them to pursue their biggest dreams in life. Encourage them to lead.

Recognize Their Gifts

Every human being has a gift and potential. It is leaders' job to help their team members discover their gifts and develop them. When you help people discover their gifts, you will encourage them greatly. People who are encouraged have hope and are positive, which will positively affect others around them.

Everyone needs AIR:

Appreciation. Tell people how much they mean to you and how appreciative you are for their contribution. You may communicate this in person, in a written message, or even by giving them a gift. Use appreciation with reserved types of individuals, as recognition may embarrass them.

Inspiration. People are inspired by what you do for them. When you support them, encourage them, and help them be accountable, and they see that you truly care about them, they will be inspired by your actions.

Recognition. Show approval in public. You may say a few words about a job well done, present people with a plaque or a certificate, or highlight them on a bulletin board or group e-mail.

The Leadership Challenge studies reveal that employees want sincere and honest appreciation more than anything else. What I have found is that personality types that are reserved prefer appreciation (a private note, word, or gift), whereas outgoing personality types thrive on public recognition. When you're generous with sincere appreciation and recognition, your team members will be inspired. When you serve them, they will be inspired. When you care for them, they will be inspired. When you love them, they will be inspired.

They will be inspired because what they want more than anything else is to matter. When you show appreciation or recognize people for a job well done, they will feel really good about themselves. When team members are inspired, they treat others really well.

Encouragement means helping others find their purpose. Just as most people don't know what their potential is, they don't know what their purpose is. When you've inspired emotional trust in someone's life, you're likely to help that person find his or her purpose.

To inspire emotional trust, follow these four steps:

1. **Demonstrate commitment to the individual.** Show people you care about them by inquiring about how they are doing as a person. Show them you care by spending time with them. Seek to understand before being understood, as the old saying goes.

2. **Invest time understanding their heart.** When investing time with people, ask them about their life. Learn about their biggest desires and biggest fears in life. Hopefully by this point, you've proved that you truly do care about them as people, not just as employees.

3. **Affirm their value.** Most human beings can't see their inherent value, much less their future potential. A great leader helps others see their potential future.

4. **Give them hope.** People lose hope because they can't see the possibilities for the problems. Give them hope by sharing inspirational stories of others who have overcome and perhaps from your own personal life if you've had to overcome difficulties.

Like the previous two steps, in order for you to *give* something, you must *have* something. In order for you to give encouragement, you must have it yourself. Winston Churchill boasted, "The key to a leader's impact is sincerity. Before he can inspire with emotion he must be swayed by it himself. Before he can move their tears his own must flow. To convince them he must himself believe." Radio personality Dave Ramsey remarked, "Surround yourself with people who add the fuel of advice and encouragement to your life."

> "Surround yourself with people who add the fuel of advice and encouragement to your life."
>
> **—DAVE RAMSEY**

Do you have others around you who encourage you as a leader? Bill Beckham, my early mentor, has been a source of encouragement for me over the years, as Rick Jones has. They've inspired emotional trust in me. Because they have demonstrated commitment to me by investing time with me and taken time to understand my heart, I have a great deal of trust for them and freely share my emotions. That's what you want for your team members. To build community, you need their emotional trust. And you can inspire that.

In order for your team members to open up about their true feelings, it's important to demonstrate your commitment to your team members by investing time with them. When I got my first business turnkey, which means the day-to-day operations no longer depended on me being there, I insisted on continuing to do a final interview with prospective employees so I could share my heart and vision for the company before hiring the applicant. My staff did all the pre-screening and the first few interviews. Although I couldn't be there to do the formal orientation, I arranged for new hires to spend their entire first day with me.

If I was driving around town on appointments, they rode with me. I just wanted them to understand my heart. I wanted to make sure they knew the vision and our values. Trust is created by investing time with one another and caring for one another.

Once you've supported someone for a period of time, and you've done it with integrity, it naturally inspires that person to trust you with his or her feelings. This gives you the opportunity to understand the person's heart and affirm the person's value. Encouraging others gives them hope.

In today's world, we must realize that the constant barrage of negative media instills fear rather than hope. The simple fact is that good news doesn't sell. And with increased competition for your mind and emotion, media outlets go to ridiculous lengths for your attention. From the time you wake up until the time you go to sleep, you're bombarded with alerts, buzzers, and notifications of "breaking news." Far too often, the stories are about yet another terror attack.

Could it be that we are afraid because we're filling our minds with negative news that discourages us rather than encouraging one another by building positive, encouraging relationships?

The point here is that everyone has fear, whether people admit it or not. However, humans are resilient, so they figure out ways to deal with fear. Unfortunately, that usually involves self-medication, pride, arrogance, denial, blame, or shame, but the fact is that deep down, most people in our society experience fear to some degree or another, and they aren't getting the encouragement they crave.

Your company can be different. You can create a sense of belonging that results in a sense of community and ultimately end up with true community. May I remind you of the benefits once more? Happy, encouraged, engaged, inspired team members who can't wait to get to work every day to implement your vision. Happier, more devoted customers, clients, members, patients, guests, or donors. Bigger profits, bigger donations, bigger outcomes.

Leaders Need Encouragement Too

As the leader, you also need to be encouraged. I'm grateful to my early mentor Bill Beckham, who continues to encourage me to this day. Over all the years I've known him, he has told me how proud he is of me and my work. Rick Jones is another one. When Rick was contemplating joining my team as a coach, he insisted on working with me for six months (without pay) before making a commitment. We traveled to leadership conferences together and shared our values on leadership and life. Bill and Rick both affirm my value. They both tell me what I'm doing is extremely valuable and important, which gives me hope for the future. If it wasn't for their mentoring, I wouldn't be writing this book right now. Only heaven knows how many people they've helped. Zig Ziglar said, "Encouragement is the fuel on which hope runs."

"Encouragement is the fuel on which hope runs."

—ZIG ZIGLAR

Every leader needs a mentor. Every leader needs hope. Every leader needs a coach who will support, encourage, and hold him or her accountable. Zig Ziglar and John Maxwell were both mentored by the late Fred Smith. Everyone needs encouragement. As you lead others into a sense of belonging and community on your journey toward true community, you'll need that encouragement. You'll need the emotional fuel as well. If you don't have fuel, you can't share it with others.

STEP 4: PRACTICE GIFT EXCHANGE

Practice gift exchange is the fourth step in building community. Each one of us has different gifts, talents, strengths, and weaknesses. Each one of us has a different personality type and a preferred way of communicating. Understanding the individual characteristics of each of your team members not only encourages each employee but it benefits the entire organization.

Most employees aren't aware of their personality types, how different people communicate, or how to develop their gifts. As you'll see in this chapter, helping your team members understand themselves and others will help them in all areas of their lives, and will therefore encourage them, which means they will be actively engaged in helping the company reach its vision.

As part of the encouragement key, practicing gift exchange is nurturing specific relationships that mutually recognize and promote one another's strengths and talents in an intentional manner. A championship team is made up of talented individuals with tremendous gifts, skills, and talents. But they win only if they communicate well and if they recognize and promote one another's gifts.

For example, Tom Brady, quarterback for the Super Bowl champion New England Patriots, has a different skill set than tight end Rob Gronkowski. Different positions require different talents. They are both extremely talented, but if they don't communicate—if each doesn't do his job—they fail together. Not only do they have to communicate, they have to support each other, encourage each other, and hold each other accountable to win consistently. We win together and we fail together. That's community.

If you think of yourself as a coach, your job as a leader is to develop your players. Leaders develop people. In an earlier chapter I quoted author Jim Collins's advice: "Get the right people on the bus, then get them in the right seat." In *Good to Great: Why Some Companies Make the Leap and Others Don't*, he offers a great illustration of building a team. Switching Brady and Gronkowski (both great talents in their own respect) to the other's seat would be disastrous and ridiculous. A leader's responsibility is to get the right person on the bus and then get him or her in the right seat.

Incidentally, one of the traits of the best companies that made the list in Collins's study in *Good to Great* was something he called Level 5 leadership. The best companies had great leadership. As a leader-coach, you'll want to know your players so you can develop them. Too often managers practice judgmental management or observational management.

Judgmental management is when a manager makes a judgment about a team member and puts the person in a box. You'll hear statements like "He's always late." The problem with judgmental management is that it doesn't put you in a good frame of mind for coaching. If you don't believe you can develop a person into the person he needs to be, then why is he on your team? And by the way, who hired that person? Judgmental management *dis*courages rather than *en*courages. It takes away courage rather than giving courage.

Observational management happens when a manager bases his or her opinions on how people do their work. It doesn't matter whether they got results. Even though the team won, they get criticized on *how* they did it. No wonder employees are disengaged! Observational management is also discouraging rather than encouraging. One of my coaching clients, the owner of an insurance company who is in his late sixties, told me how he made the winning shot for a season championship on his high school basketball team. But the coach, who in his words "didn't like me very much," still criticized how he did it! This man is almost seventy years old, and that jab still hurts!

Phenomenal leaders help their team members discover and develop their gifts. They then facilitate training to help team members develop their gifts and talents to increase their skill level. Training breeds confidence, and confident team players win the game.

> Phenomenal leaders help their team members
> discover and develop their gifts.

There's sufficient data that shows one of the most important ways to encourage and develop your team is in the area of personal development. When you help your team members understand themselves and how they communicate, help them build positive habits and better relationships, and help them reach more of their personal goals and dreams, you'll not only encourage them, you'll create a stronger team member overall.

When employees have stronger, more positive personal relationships and a more meaningful life outside of work, they'll be better, stronger, more positive team players. This type of training is not hard to obtain. It just takes the desire to do it.

Matthew Kelly captured it well in his book *The Dream Manager*. He made the point that helping employees reach their dreams in life improves the business. In the book, a Dream Manager is installed at a fictitious company. Since then, Matthew Kelly has created a Dream Manager Certification. I put two of my leaders through it, and they are helping other team members reach their dreams.

Your goal in this step of practicing gift exchange is to recognize each person's gifts as well as your own and share those gifts with one another. For example, a person who is good with finances can share that gift with others to help them learn how to better manage their finances. Another person who has a gift of connecting with others can share some of the things she does to build rapport.

Whether it's buying a house, getting their teeth fixed, taking an extended vacation, or changing a habit, people are inspired by the possibilities they see when they go through the process. We also created a Dream Board where team members can post their dreams and goals to remind themselves. This vision board gets the rest of the community involved in encouraging one another as well.

How to Develop Your Team Members

Here are some steps to take to develop your team members:

Facilitate Personality Profiles

There are many behavior assessments and personality profiles available: DISC, Myers-Briggs, Flag Pages, Birkman, and more. I personally like the DISC Model of Human Behavior created by Dr. Robert Rohm (see sidebar). DISC is easy to understand and inexpensive to use.

A POWERFUL WAY TO UNDERSTAND PEOPLE USING THE DISC PERSONALITY CONCEPT

BY ROBERT A. ROHM, PH.D.

Each Person Has Unique Personality Traits

Each person's perspective is built into who they are. Some people call it "personality," and some refer to it as "temperament."

Ever notice how different your family and friends can be from you? If you are like me, you have asked yourself, "Why did they do that?" or "What were they thinking?" The starting point of understanding people is to realize and accept one simple fact: everyone is not like you!

Have you ever said the same thing to two people and received two totally different reactions? How can saying the same words produce such different results? Each person "heard" you differently based on his or her personality style! You said the same thing, but what they "heard" was different.

Different is not bad, it is just different! A lack of understanding of ourselves and others can lead to real problems such as tension, disappointment, hurt feelings, unmet expectations, and poor communication. As you know, it is hard to work with a problem, especially if you do not understand what is going on inside the mind of another person.

There Is a Simple Way to Understand People!

The good news is that there is a simple key to understand how people behave and how they are motivated. We call the concept the DISC Model of Human Behavior. This concept will allow you to unlock the mystery behind developing good people skills and creating better relationships. You will be able to use what you learn in this introduction to reduce conflict, improve productivity, and relate with others more effectively.

Some Background on the DISC Model of Human Behavior

Twenty-four hundred years ago, scientists and philosophers, most notably Hippocrates, began to recognize and categorize differences in behavior that seemed to follow a pattern.

Since then, many psychologists and scientists have explored behavioral patterns. Dr. William Marston wrote *The Emotions of Normal People* in 1928 after earning his doctorate from Harvard University. Marston theorized that people are motivated by four intrinsic drives that direct behavioral patterns. He used four descriptive characteristics for behavioral tendencies which are represented by four letters of the alphabet: D, I, S, and C. Thus the concept of "DISC" was introduced.

Building on a "Wellness" Model

Many behavioral models focus on what is wrong with a person to identify "personality disorders." The DISC model is based on normal behavior, not abnormal behavior. DISC is a "wellness model" that is objective and descriptive rather than subjective and judgmental. Therefore, DISC is a practical way to understand yourself and those around in the common settings of everyday life.

A Positive Approach

The DISC wellness model is a good framework for understanding people. DISC should be used in a positive way to encourage a person to be his or her best—not as a way to "label" someone.

Healthy, positive relationships come from having an accurate understanding of yourself and others. DISC is a powerful tool for obtaining a new appreciation for our personality styles and their effect on our everyday lives.

We apply the DISC model with four main ideas that allow it to be used appropriately as an effective and encouraging tool:

1. We use a positive approach to highlight and encourage a person in his or her strengths.

2. We use a positive approach to address a person's possible blind spots without assuming a weakness exists.

3. We recognize that each person has a unique blend of all the major personality traits to a greater or lesser extent.

4. We recognize that behavioral patterns are fluid and dynamic as a person adapts to his or her environment.

I have a saying that, "Your strengths should carry you while your blind spots should concern you." Being able to identify and articulate your strengths can be very empowering. Being able to identify and uncover blind spots can also be very empowering! The next few pages can be the start of your own empowering discovery process.

So, now that you know where the DISC concept came from and the importance of having a positive, flexible approach, let's take a look at the Model of Human Behavior using the DISC!

The DISC Model of Human Behavior

The DISC Model of Human Behavior is based on two foundational observations about how people normally behave:

Observation #1: Some people are more outgoing, while others are more reserved. You can think of this trait as each person's "internal motor" or "pace." Some people always seem ready to "go" and "dive in" quickly. They engage their motor quickly. Others tend to engage their motor more slowly or more cautiously.

Observation # 2: Some people are more task-oriented, while others are more people-oriented. You can think of this as each person's "external focus" or "priority" that guides them. Some people are focused on getting things done (tasks); others are more tuned in to the people around them and their feelings.

With both observations, we want to emphasize that these behavioral tendencies are neither right or wrong or good or bad. They are just different. We are simply identifying normal behavior styles. People have different styles, and that is okay. We represent these two observations in Figure 7.1.

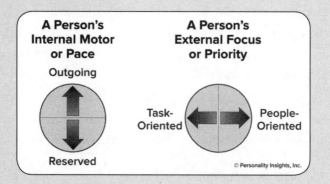

Figure 7.1   Behavioral Tendencies: Outgoing vs. Reserved
and Task-Oriented vs. People-Oriented

Four Major Personality Traits

In review, we have four behavioral tendencies to help us characterize people:

- Outgoing

- Reserved

- Task-oriented

- People-oriented

Everyone has some of all four of these tendencies at different times and in different situations. However, most people typically have one or two of these tendencies that seem to fit them well in their everyday behavior. And, on the other hand, one or two of these tendencies usually do not fit them well, and these tendencies may even seem "foreign" to their approach to life. The balance of these four tendencies shapes the way each person "sees" life and those around them. By combining the two previous diagrams, we can show four basic quadrants of the circle as shown in Figure 7.2. Thus, four basic personality traits emerge from our diagram corresponding to the four quadrants of the circle (in clockwise order):

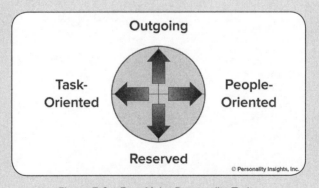

Figure 7.2   Four Major Personality Traits

- Outgoing and task-oriented (upper left quadrant)

- Outgoing and people-oriented (upper right quadrant)

- Reserved and people-oriented (lower right quadrant)

- Reserved and task-oriented (lower left quadrant)

Next, we will add descriptive terms for each of the four main personality types that emerge in the diagram. The descriptive terms will begin with D, I, S, and C.

Describing Each Personality Style

There are four different personality types with four different priorities. Notice the letters D, I, S and C appear in the four quadrants of the circle in Figure 7.3. You will also notice that descriptive terms have been added in each of the four corners of the diagram. Now we can further describe each of the four main personality styles:

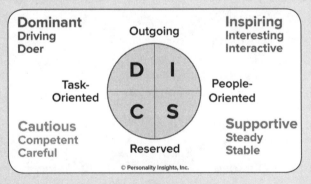

Figure 7.3   Four Personality Styles

D-I-S-C Descriptive Terms

1. **The Dominant "D" type.** An outgoing, task-oriented individual will be focused on getting things done, accomplishing tasks, getting to the bottom line as quickly as possible and "making it happen"! The key insight

in developing a relationship with this type of person is respect and results.

2. **The Inspiring "I" type.** An outgoing, people-oriented individual loves to interact, socialize, and have fun. This person is focused on what others may think of him or her. The key insight in developing a relationship with this type person is admiration and recognition.

3. **The Supportive "S" type.** A reserved, people-oriented individual will enjoy relationships, helping or supporting other people, and working together as a team. The key insight in developing a relationship with this person is friendliness and sincere appreciation.

4. **The Cautious "C" type.** A reserved, task-oriented individual will seek value, consistency, and quality information. This person focuses on being correct and accurate. The key insight in developing a relationship with this individual is trust and integrity.

Summarizing the DISC Traits

To summarize the DISC Model of Human Behavior (in clockwise order):

- D stands for the Dominant type, which is outgoing and task-oriented.

- I stands for the Inspiring type, which is outgoing and people-oriented.

- S stands for the Supportive type, which is reserved and people-oriented.

- C stands for the Cautious type, which is reserved and task-oriented.

What Is Your PQ (Personality Quotient)?

We spend years in school developing our intelligence to effectively use our mind. Developing our unique personality to effectively use our behavior is just as vital to successful living. Your intelligence quotient, or IQ, measures your intelligence. Your Personality Quotient, or PQ, refers to your ability to understand yourself and others for effective communication and teamwork. Studies have shown that technical skill, beginning with intelligence and developed through education and experience, accounts for only 15 percent of success in the workplace. The other 85 percent of workplace success comes from people skills! These skills are developed through learning better ways to behave and interact.

The Elevator Test: Which Type Are You?

The elevator doors are about to close on an eager rider who is trying to get on the elevator. Four people are already inside the elevator. One of the people in the crowded box is in a hurry and does not want to wait (outgoing and task-oriented). There is also a bubbly, energetic passenger who holds the door open while greeting the newcomer (outgoing and people-oriented). A third rider is happy either way and smiles while waiting patiently (reserved and people-oriented). The final passenger is concerned as she calculates the weight to see if the elevator can handle another person (reserved and task-oriented).

While not perfectly scientific, this scenario illustrates the Dominant (outgoing / task-oriented) person who is focused on getting somewhere fast; the Inspiring (outgoing / people-oriented) person who is energized by all the interaction; the Supportive (reserved /

people-oriented) person who reacts calmly and tries to get along regardless; and the Cautious (reserved / task-oriented) person who wants to make sure the added person doesn't exceed the weight limit! As you can see, there were four different people who responded to the same event in four very different ways!

This Is Just the Beginning!

One of the dangers of learning about DISC is that you may think you now understand all there is to know about it. We have just scratched the surface of the dynamics involved in personality styles. Did you know there are not just four personality styles? We identify 41 specific personality blends that are all very different. Even within the 41 personality blends, there can be a wide variety of nuances.

The next step is to take a personality assessment. A DISC personality profile assessment is available at http://www.howardpartridge .com/products. As I wrote in my book *Positive Personality Profiles*, "If I understand you, and you understand me, doesn't it make sense that we can work more effectively together?"

I trust this introduction will help you to experience more success in your life!

Implement Personal Development Training

There are many ways to implement a personal development program in your company. And each one of these methods is a powerful step to building community.

Here are a few ways to do it:

- **Facilitate a Growth POD.** Later in this book you'll learn how to facilitate a Growth POD. A Growth POD is a perfect environment for helping others develop themselves personally. You could choose a personal development or leadership book and go through it as a group.

- **Host a formal training.** Many of our coaching members have become certified in various training programs so that they can provide formal training in-house themselves.

- **Invite a guest speaker.** Many times, your team becomes so familiar with you as the leader or business owner that they may not value the information the way they will when you bring in an expert on the subject.

- **Use video technology.** We provide team training for some of our coaching clients via two-way videoconference. This way, our trainer can see the body language of the participants.

- **Outside training courses.** Sending team members to training is an important message that you believe in them and you are investing in them. Attending a conference or training with them is a phenomenal way to build a sense of community. And if you travel together, you can have loads of fun and really learn about one another. I've personally spent many hours on an airplane learning about one of my employees' goals and dreams.

- **Private mentoring and coaching.** Whether operating as a Dream Manager or just making yourself available to talk about dreams, goals, and personal habits, private mentoring or coaching is also a wonderful way to develop team members and build community.

  Caution: Avoid falling into counseling. Emotional problems may require therapy, and unless you are a trained therapist, it's not wise to enter that space. People may share deep hurts, past abuse, or something that goes beyond the scope of mentoring. In that case, encourage the person to get professional counseling.

To help focus your team, it's helpful to organize the areas where they can become more intentional into the following seven core categories. These categories can help as team members try to understand where they need more development. The seven core areas of life are:

1. **Personal.** This area includes hobbies, lifestyle, personal possessions, travel, and so on. A solid goal-setting program would be appropriate here as well as a program that helps your team members build better personal habits.

2. **Financial.** This area includes how team members might best manage their personal income, investing, saving, and building a net worth. At the basic level, Dave Ramsey's Financial Peace University has a kit that companies can purchase to teach financial management to individuals.

3. **Career.** This area will include specific training pertaining to a team member's job but will also include the systems we will talk about in a later chapter.

4. **Family.** This area includes how we relate to one another at home but can also include how to handle family situations while at work. Many times the family dynamics at home affect the performance of the team member. Whether it's excessive phone calls or text messages or relationship difficulties, helping a team member build healthier relationships at home can have a far-reaching impact beyond the work environment. It can literally change a family's legacy.

5. **Physical.** This area involves eating right, exercising, and managing energy. Many people are overweight because they have never been trained on nutrition or haven't made it a priority in their lives. Going beyond just installing exercise equipment or buying a membership to the local gym, you could invite people to learn about nutrition and exercise.

   A couple of years ago, many of our team members joined a health program at the same time. By going through it together, they supported one another, encouraged one another, and helped one another be accountable.

   Physically unhealthy team members equals more sick time, less focus, less energy, less production, more stress, and the greater possibility of a valuable employee having a heart attack or stroke, which leaves your company in a difficult situation.

6. **Mental.** This area involves learning, dealing with stress, and building emotional intelligence. This could include building winning relationships, communicating, doing focus or memory exercises, and even learning specific skills. The more mental energy people have, the more focus they have and the more effective they can be. The more positive, supportive, and encouraging they are, the stronger the team will be.

7. **Spiritual.** This is the area of faith. I'll leave this one to you and your culture.

Discover Gifts and Talents

In addition to DISC, there are a number of assessments that can help you and your team members discover their unique talents. I like The DISC Model of Human Behavior because it is simple and it is easier for team members to remember their profile. However, using other assessment tools can deepen your understanding of yourself and your team. I suggest going through each one of them to find the one that best suits you and your team.

Jodi Carroll, a brilliant leadership practitioner, helped me compile a list of some of the most popular personality assessments (see sidebar).

POPULAR PERSONALITY ASSESSMENTS
RESEARCH DONE BY ALEXANDRA ZIGLAR

MBTI (Myers Briggs Type Indicator)

The MBTI is a personality assessment created by Isabel Briggs Myers and her mother, Katherine Briggs, based on Carl G. Jung's three personality preferences: Extraverted (E) vs. Introverted (I), Sensing (S) vs. Intuition (N), and Thinking (T) vs. Feeling (F); Myers and Briggs created a fourth personality preference: Judging (J) vs. Perceiving (P).

Essentially, these four basic personality preferences are referred to as *dichotomies*, meaning an individual exerts a stronger tendency toward one of the personality traits in an either/or scenario. For example, individuals behave either extraverted or introverted; they either enjoy being involved in group settings and are energized by spending time with people or they prefer to spend time alone in self-reflection and explore their imagination.

Additionally, individuals receive information either by *sensing* or by *intuition*; they either prefer to interpret new information as a matter of fact by sensing observations in the external world (sounds, appearance, touch, smell) or they prefer to interpret new information through their intuition based on observations in their internal world—they use patterns, symbols, possibilities, and ideas as a connecting tool for understanding the bigger picture of the information presented.

Further, individuals prefer to make decisions either on a basis of *thinking* or on a basis of *feeling*; they either take an impersonal and objective approach, considering the logicality of the decision, or they choose to consider the emotions of others and take an empathetic approach before they make a decision. Finally, individuals prefer to implement new information by either *judging* or *perceiving*; they either choose to act on new information by using past experiences as a guide for creating an organized plan of action or they accept new information as detached from prior experiences and are not concerned with creating a structured plan of action—instead, they are flexible and easily adaptable to new information.

The MBTI assessment involves asking the participant questions relevant to each dichotomy, and a personality type is drawn from a dominance found in each trait. Specifically, from a bank of 16 possible personality types, an individual is given an acronym derived from each trait's designated letter to form a personality type. For example, a person with an acronym of ISTJ is introverted, receives information by sensing observations of the outside world, makes decisions based on logic, and implements new information by judging past experience and creating an organized plan of action. The overall purpose of the MBTI is to gain insight into individuals' communication style, skill sets, and strengths and weaknesses and, more important, how they respond and think about new information. The MBTI assessment has many purposes: to help develop one's team by practicing effective communication techniques unique to each member's communication style, to develop leadership skills among one's team by identifying each member's strengths and weaknesses, to avoid conflict and manage stress by understanding each individual's working style and how the person reacts to deadlines and pressure, and finally, to help individuals set goals by assessing how each person naturally makes and implements decisions.

StrengthsFinder

StrengthsFinder is an assessment that helps individuals identify their strengths and talents through a series of 177 questions. The questions are arranged by theme and organized in pairings in which individuals identify the statement that best characterizes their personality and then rank the relatability of the statement to their personality type. For example, the theme of Harmony might include two statements that read: "I enjoy helping others" and "I like it when others help me." An individual ranks the accurateness of each descriptor in relation to his or her personality on a continuum of Strongly Describes Me (for one statement), Neutral, and Strongly Describes Me (for the other statement). The strongest pairings are tallied by theme (usually the top five themes) to determine an individual's areas of strength, and strategies are delegated to these top-ranked themes. Strategies include practical applications and knowledge required to maximize each strength. The overall purpose of the assessment is to provide individuals with the knowledge they need to transform raw talent into mastered skills.

Interestingly, the philosophy behind this assessment aims to focus solely on individual strengths and disregard weaknesses. The founders of this assessment believed that positive psychology was a crucial component of making individuals believe they have talents ready to be utilized. They believed individuals are endowed with raw talent, and it is only a matter of awakening that inner talent with refined skills and practice. Overall, the assessment helps individuals become introspective and gain insight into their strengths so they can begin their journey of personal development.

Birkman

The Birkman Method is a behavioral assessment that measures people's needs, evaluates people's personality and perceptions in social settings, draws a correlation between attitude and performance in a work environment, and provides participants with career choices unique to their working styles. Specifically, the questionnaire includes 298 questions ranging from true-false to multiple choice, and each question aims to assess an individual's behavior in the work environment. The Need aspect of the assessment identifies an individual's needs and composes a plan of action for fulfilling them. The Birkman Method teaches that once individuals' needs are fulfilled, they are more likely to stay motivated and on task, increasing their efficiency at work. The Personality and Perception aspect of the assessment evaluates how individuals think about new information and their interactions with staff members. The Birkman Method teaches that once individuals understand how others perceive the world, they are more likely to remain open-minded, contributing to a more harmonious staff environment. The Behavioral and Occupational aspect of the assessment focuses on how people's attitudes affect their performance and satisfaction in the workplace. The Birkman Method teaches that it is important to have a work culture in which employees and managers work together and an environment that keeps employees interested in the task at hand—the assessment provides participants with a list of occupations unique to their specified interests.

Johnson O'Connor Aptitude Assessment

The Johnson O'Connor Aptitude Assessment measures an individual's aptitude by having a participant perform a number of hands-on tasks and memory games under the monitor of a proctor. A participant may be asked to solve puzzles, listen to music, build block towers, memorize visual patterns, and so on. The assessment is not concerned with identifying an individual's personality traits but rather with assessing his or her natural talents or abilities. The founders of the assessment believed that personality assessments are often too biased since the individual taking the assessment is evaluating his strengths and weaknesses based on his perception of himself. Therefore, an assessment that requires a proctor or an administrator to evaluate the aptitude of an individual is more likely to eliminate any biased results. The overall purpose of the assessment is to help people discover their natural abilities and then provide occupations that highlight and use those natural abilities so that individuals can enjoy their chosen career field.

RIASEC

RIASEC is an acronym for what John Holland refers to as six personality traits: Realistic, Investigative, Artistic, Social, Enterprising, and Conventional. The RIASEC assessment is a personality evaluation that groups people's personalities into six basic career fields; this helps people find a job that is suitable to their personality. The assessment involves 48 questions in which participants rate their likability of a given statement. For example, a statement might read: "I prefer performing detailed and structured work," and the individual would be asked to rate his or her likability of this statement on a scale of *dislike, slightly enjoy, slightly dislike, neither like or dislike, slightly enjoy,* and *enjoy.*

Unlike other personality assessments, RIASEC directly appropriates personality types into career fields. For example, the Realistic personality type enjoys working with tools, likes to complete detailed mechanical projects, and typically avoids working with people. The Investigative personality type enjoys analytical work such as solving math equations and conducting scientific experiments and prefers to present information in a clear, precise manner. The Artistic personality type enjoys participating in activities that require self-expression and creativity such as dance, theater, music, or art and typically avoids activities that are repetitive and require structure or organization. The Social personality type enjoys interacting with people and performing service work such as nursing, counseling, or nonprofit roles and typically avoids using machinery and other mechanical tools. The Enterprising personality type is charismatic and skilled at persuading and convincing others; people with this personality type typically enjoy leadership roles and challenging themselves. Finally, the Conventional personality type enjoys routine work that is characterized by systems and procedure; people with this personality type feel uncomfortable without a specific plan to follow and need order to be successful.

Sources: http://www.myersbriggs.org/my-mbti-personality-type/mbti-basics /preferences.htm; https://www.cpp.com/products/mbti/index.aspx; http://www .humanmetrics.com/personality/type; http://strengths.gallup.com/110440 /about-strengthsfinder-20.aspx; http://strengths.gallup.com/private/Resources /CSFTechnicalReport031005.pdf; https://birkman.com/assessment-solutions /the-birkman-method/; http://www.jocrf.org/ing; https://www.careerkey.org /choose-a-career/holland-personality-types.html#.WThaXfryuqA; http://personality -testing.info/tests/RIASEC/

Develop the Team Professionally

The final way to develop your team is to find ways to help team members grow in their areas of expertise. Growing and developing their skills to the top level of their disciplines will greatly strengthen the team. In addition to technical training, consider leadership training as a path for professional growth.

In order to develop leaders, people need to know how to lead. Most managers fall into the "command and control" trap, but when you have them trained in the right kind of leadership philosophy, you can replace yourself in many areas and you now have people who can lead new teams to grow your organization.

It's worth repeating that technical skills and job skills do not translate into leadership skills. Everyone in your company is a leader because everyone has influence in someone else's life. When existing or emerging managers learn how to communicate better and become more effective at coaching, teaching, and facilitating, you'll have set your company up for future growth and will deal a tremendous blow to disengagement.

Many business owners don't make this kind of investment in their employees—in time or money—because they fear they may invest heavily in team members only to have them quit. Although it's always possible for that to happen, here's a great question to ask yourself: "Would it be better to train them and lose them or to not train them and keep them?" If you don't have a training budget, start with this book and our free resources and do a POD in your company.

By investing in developing your players and providing a supportive, encouraging environment, you'll not only retain more of them, but they'll be much more engaged and productive.

Practicing Gift Exchange Externally

As with the other steps to building community, there's a component of this step outside your company. Practicing gift exchange outside your company means that you add people to your network who have gifts you don't have.

As a leader of your business or manager in your organization, the one thing that will make all the difference in your performance is having the right community around you. We all need coaches, mentors, and people in our personal and professional lives who have gifts we don't have.

We need people to shore up our weaknesses. My friend Ellen Rohr is a good example of this. She had financial systems that I needed. Although Rick Jones is now on my team, he was a resource for me on the outside first—a phenomenal trainer with impressive skills in coaching that I didn't have.

I stay engaged with books, audio and video programs, workshops, conferences, and training sessions. To be a phenomenal leader, you must develop yourself first before you can develop others.

Every phenomenal successful leader has a coach, a mentor, or, in the best case, a community of coaches, mentors, and peers who provide support, encouragement, and accountability. In the next chapter, we'll dive into the subject of accountability.

STEP 5: INVITE OPENHEARTED ENCOUNTERS

Now that we've covered the first two keys—support and encouragement—and the first four of the Six Steps, it's time to talk about the third key: accountability. Once you've served others and encouraged them over a period of time, the possibility of an accountability relationship opens up. The kind of accountability I'm talking about is welcomed accountability.

Far too often, business owners or managers try to hold people accountable without a relationship. When accountability is done right, people will *want* to be accountable. They will *want* to be better. There's a big difference between forcing someone to be accountable

Far too often, business owners or managers try to hold people accountable without a relationship.

and inviting someone into accountability through support and encouragement. As the old saying goes, "Nobody cares how much you know, until they know how much you care." Zig added "about them." "Nobody cares how much you know, until they know how much you care *about them*."

Accountability is much more effective and lasting when it's built on a foundation of care and concern. Once you've invested in others by supporting and serving them and you've built a stronger bond by inspiring emotional trust and practiced gift exchange, the foundation exists to move into this level of relationship, which is the most meaningful and most transformational level of all.

Accountability is much more effective and lasting when it's built on a foundation of care and concern.

This doesn't mean that you don't hold your people accountable to do the things they are supposed to do if you don't have that kind of relationship. You do. But accountability without a relationship doesn't last. No one wants team members who do only what they're supposed to do when someone is watching. The kind of accountability that builds community is a different kind of accountability.

The dictionary's definition of accountability is to "account for one's actions." In *Thou Shalt Prosper*, Rabbi Daniel Lapin gives the Hebrew definition of *accountability* as "focusing on what's important now." For our purposes, we will define accountability as helping others become the persons they need to be. To help your team members develop themselves, grow to their full potential, and be as valuable as they can to the community, you need to build a culture of accountability that says, "I care enough about you to help you become the person you want to be."

Step back and think about how deep that is for a moment. That you, as a business owner or leader, can literally help someone change his or her life. You—yes, you—can help people become the person they need to be to prosper in life. That's community. The result is you'll have team members who love you and are committed to you, because you loved them and were committed to them first. I've personally witnessed this among my own team members as well as client companies.

Accountability in this sense is the deepest level of relationship and the most powerful. There is no greater connection than true love. Phenomenal leaders love others. Of course, as mentioned in an earlier chapter, the word *love* has many definitions, but in this case, we define love as commitment. Phenomenal leaders are committed to their team members, which when done with sincerity will create a mutual commitment from team members. Only your very best team members will move up to this level of relationship. People who aren't interested in community will self-eliminate themselves along the way. This should not alarm you but should comfort you, as you'll be left with "A players" who will attract others just like them.

As with the other keys, in order to offer this level of accountability to someone else, you must live it yourself. Phenomenal leaders live a lifestyle of accountability. That is, you have to take responsibility for your own actions, be respectful to your team members, be open to them, and allow yourself to be vulnerable. You have to be willing to admit when you're wrong, confess that you don't have all the answers, and ask your team for feedback on how you're doing as a leader.

Phenomenal leaders live a lifestyle of accountability.

If you cheat on your taxes or live a life without integrity, you'll attract others who do the same. At the same time, understanding that we are all flawed human beings, confessing our weaknesses to one another, and having people around us who love us enough to walk through our difficulties with forgiveness is refreshing and liberating. But it is something that most leaders unfortunately never experience.

One of the reasons for this is the overall lack of accountability in our culture. It's unfortunate that accountability, whether on an individual basis or on a corporate level, is sorely lacking in our society today. Whether it's corporate scandals such as Enron or personal greed as was the case with Bernie Madoff, our cultural attitude today seems to be "take care of number one."

As for the lack of personal responsibility, one has to look no further than the case of Ethan Couch. In 2013, 17-year-old Ethan Couch killed four people while driving drunk. He was driving on a restricted license and speeding in a residential area when he lost control, colliding with a group of people assisting another driver with a disabled SUV. A total of nine people were injured. One of the passengers in Couch's truck was completely paralyzed.

His attorneys successfully pleaded "affluenza"—a condition theoretically created by mass consumerism, and in this case "the inability to understand the consequences of one's actions because of financial privilege."

The judge gave him probation rather than prison time, which created an understandable public outcry. But that was just the beginning of the Ethan Couch story. When his probation officer was unable to contact him, a national manhunt eventually found him having a good time in Mexico, in hiding with the aid of his mother.

Our cultural attitude today seems to be that if you can beat a speeding ticket (even if you are guilty) or get away with doing something wrong, it's a badge of honor. And whatever a person does, many think it should be without consequence. It's ironic to me that people want to keep their lives so private and free of judgment, yet we live such public lives on social media.

The lack of perspective that comes from the lack of accountability has created a host of problems in management, but the fact remains that at every human being's core is the desire to be loved, accepted, and important. Support, encouragement, and accountability helps phenomenal leaders help others fulfill that need.

The fifth step, invite "openhearted encounters," means to embrace the power of transparent experiences with faithful friends—permitting them to speak honestly and ask piercing questions.

At this point in the process, a leader and his or her team members should have a strong enough relationship to speak openly and honestly with one another even though doing so can make them vulnerable. This is admittedly a difficult step to achieve because many people, having been mistreated, taken advantage of, and betrayed by others in the past, are understandably unwilling to put themselves in this kind of situation.

However, it is only by making ourselves vulnerable that we make ourselves accountable to others. For that reason, leaders who want their team members to be accountable must first exhibit accountability and vulnerability themselves. One thing is clear: people cling to authentic leadership.

Leaders who want their team members to be accountable must first exhibit accountability and vulnerability themselves.

Inviting "openhearted encounters" helps each of us become the person we need to be, and leaders who help their team members accomplish that will not only be followed but will be loved as well. Creating these kinds of relationships is also an important element of promoting community in an organization.

In this sense it means providing feedback to your team members so they can become the people they need to become. In practical terms, being accountable means being true to your own values—to what you believe is important in life. When people truly believe in the values they have adopted, they automatically do the things they are supposed to do and therefore have the outcome they want. Humans tend to do what we value, and we value what we do.

Accountability is about building character. People's character is who they truly are, and our values make up our character. Patrick Lencioni talks about aspirational values versus actual values. Our actual values are who we are now. Aspirational values are who we want to become—as a company or as an individual.

Constant constructive feedback helps us become who we want to become. Chuck Coonradt shares in his book *The Game of Work* that good leaders give constant feedback. Imagine a football game with no scoreboard. How would you know whether you're winning or not? Imagine having to play the entire game without any time-outs. You could never get feedback from one another to adjust your game plan.

Another lesson comes from the book *Beyond Entrepreneurship* by Jim Collins and the late William C. Lazier:

> Human beings perform better when they have a positive self-image, and psychologists in a variety of experiments have found that people's performance—objectively measured—improves or declines depending on the type of feedback they get. Positive feedback tends to improve performance, whereas negative feedback tends to decrease performance. Yet, all too often, people get precious little feedback from company leaders—positive or negative. The absence of feedback sends a message: We don't care about you. And when people feel you don't care about them, they're not going to give you their best effort. Why should they?

They continue, "There's nothing inconsistent between having a close-knit 'family' feeling and weeding out poor performers."

The Character Mirror

Accountability is feedback. Imagine accountability as a mirror. It's a mirror to see who you're becoming. Therefore, accountability is a "character mirror," so to speak. There's a social media meme that depicts a kitten looking in a large mirror. But instead of seeing himself as a kitten, the reflection reveals a huge, powerful, courageous lion. This is what accountability should do for people. It should help them see who they can become.

In the previous chapter, we talked about discovering others' gifts and talents. Those gifts are developed further through this step. And if you want to build true community in your organization, you have to determine the values that will guide your community and make sure that every member of your team, every individual in the community, operates by those values. It is only when the members of your team are accountable in this way that they, and the company, will be in a position to achieve their respective destinies.

The idea of living this way may seem overwhelming and maybe a little dangerous, but I know from my own experience that it's only by doing so that you will be able to develop true community in your organization. Only by living an accountable life yourself, both personally and professionally—and the two are connected—will you be able to promote that value in your organization.

To break this down, accountability helps us do a number of things:

Account for Our Actions

This is the most obvious use of accountability, but again many managers try to force accountability without the trust and respect that comes from establishing a solid relationship. Of course people should do their jobs. That isn't in question here. How people go about accomplishing their daily work is the point.

If I'm being accountable for my actions, I must confess the truth. I may not like the fact that I missed the mark, but in order to build my character and perform better, I must reflect on what went well and what didn't. Looking into the character mirror allows us to reflect on who we are becoming.

Develop Our Gifts and Talents

Every human being has unique talents, but those gifts and talents have to be developed. Good coaches help their team members recognize their gifts and talents through support and encouragement. Those gifts and talents are developed through accountability as players get feedback on their performance.

When I speak of performance here, I don't mean just performance in the tactical sense but also in the sense of living out the values that have been established. If one of the values is honesty, I can reflect on how honest I have been, for example.

Focus on What's Important Now

In order to "account" for something, we have to focus on it. We have to shed light on it. Accountability causes us to shine a spotlight on our behavior and then dig deeper to find out what the motivation for that behavior is.

Stay Committed to Our Values

In essence, accountability ensures our commitment to the vision and values we have adopted for our lives and for the organization. If you haven't selected your aspirational values, you can explore that in Chapter 10, "Develop Your Community Systems."

Commit to One Another

Accountability is the third and final key to building true community. After all, what kind of community would we be if we weren't committed deeply to one another? It is through the accountability process that our character grows. We literally become a different person. The accountability process brings us face-to-face with our values.

How to Coach Without Drama

As you follow these steps, you'll discover a lot about your team. Once you settle on your vision and values and you begin to engage your team, you'll find out who is committed and who isn't. Once you've done your part as a leader—provided the resources to do the job, outlined the vision, and opened up the lines of communication—you can properly coach someone who misses the mark. And you can do it without creating drama.

Many business owners and managers don't do a great job of coaching someone who misses the mark. Calling someone out is awkward and uncomfortable. However, when support, encouragement, and accountability are part of the culture, when you've followed the first four steps of creating a culture of community, and when you've outlined your systems, coaching becomes much easier.

Following the logic—you've hired the right people with the right values, you've trained them on your systems, and you've supported them and encouraged them—an accountability session should feel natural. Accountability must be something that is part of your everyday culture. When it is, you can avoid the awkward, uncomfortable feeling of having to scold someone. When you constantly give feedback in a positive way, the conversation is natural.

Keep in mind that a leader is a coach—and a good coach asks good questions. My goal when coaching someone is to never make a statement. Done properly, you can coach someone to success simply by asking questions.

The following questions cut to the chase:

1. Do you know what to do?

2. Do you know how to do it?

3. Do have the tools and resources you need?

The goal of a coaching session is simply to determine whether you're dealing with an *aptitude* issue or an *attitude* issue. In other words, is it a skill problem or a motivation problem? Of course, the first step is making sure that the structure of your organization isn't broken or this employee doesn't have so much added to her plate that she's drowning. Assuming that the job can be done in the way it is designed to be done and this person has been trained to do it right, the goal of a coaching session is simply to find out if the team member is capable of doing it or if the person just doesn't want to do it. Team members shouldn't be released from training until they have shown that they can do the job successfully, so that would leave only one reason they are not doing it: they aren't engaged. The question is why.

A simple question I like to ask is, "Are we still the right fit for you?" Notice I didn't say, "You're not the right fit for us." Not everyone may want to go with you when you have a big vision and you want to build community in your business. You can respect team members and give them dignity by phrasing the question that way. And notice that I use a *question* rather than a statement. Sometimes people join the team with a great amount of zeal but lose interest. If that's the case, let them decide to go somewhere else. Can you see how simply asking questions helps them make the decision?

Leaders Need Openhearted Encounters Too

In order for us to give proper feedback to our team, to hold them accountable to the values we've adopted, and to invite them into openhearted encounters, we must be vulnerable enough to enter that space as leaders ourselves.

In Chapter 3, I shared how I had an openhearted encounter with my mentor when I was having trouble with my business partnerships. I didn't like his response, but I knew what he said was true. Sometimes the truth hurts. In an old preacher's words, "Truth without love is brutal. Love without truth is sentimental." We must tell the truth in love, and we must allow others to tell us the truth. John Gardner wrote in *On Leadership*, "Pity the leader who is caught between unloving critics and uncritical lovers." The accountability level is about telling people the truth in a loving manner.

When you love people, you're committed to them. You're committed to them even when they disappoint you. You're committed to them even when they fail. You're committed to the relationship. In a marriage ceremony, the bride and groom vow their commitment and dedication "for better, for worse, for richer, for poorer, in sickness and in health." That's real love. That's real commitment.

If we define love as a commitment and we are committed to our team members and they are committed to us, we provide the opportunity for "openhearted encounters." Being accountable means surrounding ourselves with faithful friends who care more about our long-term success as a human being than about short-term profits or what they can get from the relationship.

True community means you have people around you who tell you the truth even when it hurts. It may take a while to get to this point in a relationship and with your team members, but it is possible, and the rewards are worth the climb.

Too many leaders surround themselves with yes-men. In a seminar I attended, when Atlanta-based pastor Andy Stanley talked about accountability, he referenced how King David in the Bible was surrounded by yes-men. He questioned where the accountability was when David had Bathsheba's husband killed in battle to hide his adultery with her and pointed out that David might not have fallen had he surrounded himself with faithful friends who were willing to hold him accountable.

My personal view is that humans are special creations with many gifts and talents, but imperfect. Speaker Darren Hardy describes this paradox as being "flawsome," which means awesome and flawed all at the same time. We are all *flawsome*; therefore, on the one hand there is great hope for us. On the other hand, we need faithful friends to keep us focused on who we are becoming.

American legend Zig Ziglar would not have become the man he became had it not been for a man named P. C. Merrell. Mr. Merrell was a trainer in the sales organization Zig worked for selling cookware door-to-door. Mr. Merrell was highly respected by Zig and therefore could speak into his life. An openhearted encounter took place one day as Mr. Merrell pulled Zig aside during a training session and gave him some very tough advice: "Zig, I've never seen such a waste. You have so much talent. I believe if you went to work on a regular schedule, you could be a great one in our organization."

And a great one Zig did become. When he passed away in November 2012, it was national news. One study estimated that Zig touched a quarter of a billion lives through his many books and audio programs. It was an openhearted encounter that got his attention. But he would not have "taken the medicine," so to speak, if he did not have respect for Mr. Merrell and if Mr. Merrell had not added that he could be a "great one." Had Merrell left it at "I've never seen such a waste," Zig would have been discouraged rather than encouraged.

My wife and I have been married for 33 years. But there was a season when we didn't see eye to eye on things. We didn't agree on how to raise our son, what church should look like, and how to best handle our finances. These are all normal things that people go through, and void of community, many marriages end up in divorce. My brother and his wife happened to be in town one weekend when my wife and I were at our lowest point.

My brother and I had an "openhearted encounter" over breakfast as he asked, "Do you love her?" That was a really good question—one that haunted me. Finally I responded with, "Describe love." I came to believe that love is commitment, and I made a commitment to my wife when I married her. Therefore, I would serve her and learn how to communicate with her. Today, many years later, we enjoy a wonderful life together. That breakfast conversation was a turning point for our marriage.

I had many openhearted encounters with a man I hired to be my coach in 2009. It all started when I arrived in Clearwater, Florida, to speak at a convention. I went out to the beach to get some sun and to clear my mind. It was a brilliant day. The sky was deep blue without a cloud to be seen—the seagulls were calling, and the water was gently lapping up onto the shore. It was serene.

But the scene in my mind was not so pristine. I was frustrated because my coaching business, Phenomenal Products, was stuck. It wasn't growing, and I didn't know how to take it to the next level. I felt confused and disoriented, and I even considered quitting. I was searching for a gift from the sea, which I had often received when walking the beach.

I just didn't know what to do. I felt that I needed someone who had already done what I wanted to do, or at least who had been with someone who had done what I wanted to do. Talking out loud to myself, I said, "I've *gotta* find *someone* to help me."

I kept pacing . . . "*Who* is this person who can help me?" I scanned the names that came to mind . . . "Nope, I'm not sure I can trust that person . . . Nope . . . that one doesn't have the values I have . . . Nope, this other one would probably take advantage of the situation." (I hadn't yet built a strong relationship with Ziglar.)

At that moment, my cell phone rang. It was Mark Ehrlich. I had first met Mark a couple of years earlier when he came to Houston with Michael Gerber when Michael spoke at my conference. I picked them up at the airport in Houston, and it was cold that day. They both had long black coats on, and Michael was wearing a black hat.

When Mark introduced himself, he looked at me with a very serious look and handed me his business card: "Chief Negotiator for Michael E. Gerber." Now, this was someone I didn't even want to get *near*. I figured just being *around* the guy would cost me money!

I picked up the phone. "Howard, I'd like to get together with you to see what you're up to. . . . Okay, well, why don't you come down here to the beach? We'll grab a couple o' chairs and sit and talk. . . ."

"I'm not dressed for the beach" he shot back gruffly. "I'm wearing black pants, black shoes, a black shirt. Not exactly beach attire."

I'm thinking to myself "Who comes to the beach dressed like *that?*"

I responded, "Okay . . . tell you what, there's a little tiki bar area near the building and they've got some umbrellas. I'll meet you up there, and that way, I can still be in the sun and have my toes in the sand, and you can be in the shade. And by the way, take your shoes off for cryin' out loud. You're at the *beach!*"

"Okay, Howard," said Mark, chuckling slightly.

During our little tiki bar chat, I began to realize that Mark might be the gift from the sea I was looking for. After all, he had been with Michael Gerber on and off since 1977, and he represented speakers. So I invited him to sit in on one of the presentations I was doing the next day. He agreed to come, so the next day, Mark showed up in my seminar room (wearing all black again), and he sat in the back corner of the room and opened his little black Moleskine notebook.

During my talk, Mark hardly even looked up. He didn't seem to even be paying attention. He was writing the whole time. Working on something, I supposed. No affirmations. No nods. Nothing. Head down, writing. The *entire* time.

When I finished my talk, he started heading for the door. He was leaving! I thought, "This is weird," so I hurried to the door to catch up with him and asked, "Mark, how was my talk?"

He replied, "I've got four pages of notes . . ."

"Great!" I joyfully responded. Then he finished his sentence: ". . . of things you *should* have done but *didn't* do!" Ouch!

I ended up hiring Mark to coach me, and he started coming to all of my seminars. He sat at the back of the room (wearing all black of course), writing in his little black notebook. I'm sure my community wondered why Darth Vader was there. He was the mystery man in black who sat in the corner in the back of the room writing in his little black notebook.

After every event, he asked me why I didn't do this and why I didn't do that. Then he berated me for not doing what I should have done. Instead of calling him my mentor, I started calling him my *tor-mentor*.

Every week we had an accountability call, and the Tormentor in Black, Darth Vader, would let me have it. On one of our weekly calls, I had just done a program in Pennsylvania and had decided to drive through Princeton, New Jersey, on the way to see my in-laws who live in New Jersey.

It was a crisp, sunny morning, and as I was driving along in the rental car I imagined stopping in for a cappuccino and strolling along the little shops in Princeton—but instead I was on the phone with the "tor-mentor." He railed on me as the gorgeous views went by, and instead of getting a cappuccino, I got a stern lecture by Mark about not implementing the things I should have implemented in the seminar.

As a result of the accountability in the form of openhearted encounters with Mark, I went on to write books (something Mark made me do), and I pursued a stronger relationship with Michael Gerber and Ziglar, something I might not have done otherwise. My weekly accountability call with him was exactly what I needed to take my business to the next level.

I would never have become the person I needed to become without the accountability I got from Mark. He helped me realize that I had gifts I wasn't using. He saw my potential. Even though I wasn't who I needed to be yet, he knew who I *could* be. Mark helped me become the person I needed to be by holding up the character mirror to show me who I could be.

Openhearted encounters help us see things in a way we haven't seen them before. They give us the jolt we sometimes need when we get lulled into a values challenge. My friend Jerry Wiles told me once, "Great leaders help people think about things they haven't thought of before."

True success is simply *becoming* the person you were created to be. You will not become the person you were created to be without accountability. You will not become the person you were created to be outside of true community. Every human being has a gift. Accountability through openhearted encounters helps you discover who you are. Accountability helps you develop that gift. Accountability gives you the feedback you need. It helps you see yourself in the mirror.

Mark helped me realize my gift. He helped me see my strengths. He helped me find my purpose. He helped me realize that Phenomenal Products is not a job I'm doing. It's not a business that I'm running. It's a calling.

Who's helping you be accountable? Who's helping you discover your gift and calling? Who's helping you develop your gift? I got debt free by getting my business finances in order. That came with accountability from Ellen Rohr and Scott Zack. I got healthy by having a coach. I got unhealthy by firing my coach. I got healthy again by getting a coach.

We all need a coach, a consultant, a mentor, maybe even a tormentor if you're hardheaded like me. We need someone in each area of our lives to become the person we were created to be.

We live in a culture that despises accountability. A rich kid who kills a bunch of people driving drunk pleads "affluenza." No accountability. Enron. No accountability. Bernie Madoff. No accountability. Politicians. No accountability. When it comes to the issues of the day, we shout and scream at one another on social media. We need true community to become the best versions of ourselves.

What about your team members? Who are they becoming? They want to be phenomenally successful in all areas of life. As a business owner, CEO, or manager, you can have more influence in their lives than anyone else *if* you build community in your organization.

Your team members need accountability to become the people they need to be, but you cannot expect them to be accountable if you aren't accountable. Remember that humans are more fractured today than ever before. They've been vulnerable and have been hurt by others in an authority position. It may take a while to turn the tide. How do you do that? Create the most phenomenal community experience ever.

What about your customers, clients, patients, members, or guests? Marketing genius Seth Godin says, "Help your customers become the person they want to be." How do you do that? Create the most phenomenal community experience ever in your business, and people will want to *belong* to your community. Who does your client want to become?

One of our coaching members, an architect, recently put on her testimonial form that our coaching community "saved her marriage." She wanted to be a successful wife. The community helped her become a better wife.

When you become a phenomenal leader, you'll love others. And because of that, I believe you'll inspire your team, wow your customers, and make bigger profits.

STEP 6: BUILD GROWTH PODS

CHAPTER

The sixth and final step in building community involves developing small groups I call PODS, which stands for Power of Discovery Systems. A Growth POD is a small group that meets on a regular basis that not only helps move individuals toward true accountability but also helps spread community throughout the organization.

The purpose of the POD is to foster more effective communication. Over time these groups can move people from a sense of community to a true community experience of belonging and transformation. Unlike what happens in a traditional meeting, in which one person speaks to the group, interaction is encouraged in a POD meeting. These purpose-minded life support groups can be used for almost any reason—to reach company goals, keep a project moving forward, achieve personal goals, change habits, or develop members' skills or gifts.

The purpose of the POD is to foster more effective communication.

As I mentioned in an earlier chapter, PODS, typically made up of seven to nine individuals, are designed to allow participants to discover what they need to do or who they need to become rather than being taught (or, worse, *told*). This is particularly important in today's society because people tend to bristle when you tell them what to do, and PODS enable team members to discover important concepts on their own. And when people discover something themselves, they feel a sense of ownership, which makes it more likely that they will implement it. And when they do take action, they do it with a sense of purpose. In this chapter, you'll learn why PODS work, what kind of PODS you need, and how to facilitate a Growth POD properly.

Going back to my church experience, where I first began to think about this idea of community, I saw a major difference between the large group meeting and the small group meeting.

In a large group setting, one person speaks to an audience, but it's only one-way information. Without feedback you don't know whether your message is getting across or not. Continuing with the theme I laid out early in the book that "leadership is effectively communicating your vision," the fact is that a large group meeting isn't the most effective way to communicate. Small groups are.

But just having small groups is not the answer. Properly *facilitating* the group with a specific purpose in mind is the key to being effective. All too often, regardless of the type of meeting, the leader tends to do all the talking, and this is a mistake. One-way information doesn't transform. To make matters worse, often the leader isn't a very good speaker! Community isn't about small groups—it's about developing meaningful relationships. However, small groups, effectively facilitated, are a powerful tool in doing so.

The following material will show you an easy, effective way to communicate that doesn't involve speaking to large groups, although it would be wise for any leader to develop his or her public speaking skills. The purpose of a large group is to inspire, to celebrate, and to make general announcements. For example, The Richards Group in Dallas, the largest advertising agency in the United States, has over 700 employees, and it designed its building so that the energetic 83-year-old founder, Stan Richards, could face the entire team at once. It all happens from a catwalk that looks down on the most important space in the building to Stan: the stairway.

In the middle of the building is a wide stairway that zigzags from the bottom floor to the top floor. Employees can simply make their way to the middle of their respective floor and pile onto the wide stairway and fill in around the railings where everyone can see one another.

This is "community central," where good and bad news is shared and where new clients or prospects are introduced. When I visited the company, I was on a tour with about 120 people in our group. We joined Stan on the massive catwalk and enjoyed poems, songs, and creative presentations from the award-winning team of writers and producers that filled the stairway. It was a very effective presentation.

But of course, as with any meeting, the "meeting after the meeting" is the one that really counts. This is the meeting that happens around the proverbial "watercooler" right after the big meeting—in other words, a *small group* that gathers to search for the real meaning of what was said. Fortunately for Stan Richards, the watercooler talk mirrors the phenomenal culture of community he has successfully transferred. His vision and values are clearly seen throughout the ranks. Emily, our 30-year-old tour guide, told exciting tales about the culture and history of The Richards Group. She shared how the company had sent her to present to clients when she was only 19. Later on as we gathered for another large group session—a lecture from Stan on the company's values—we heard the same stories we had heard from Emily earlier.

The "meeting after the meeting" is the one that really counts.

Even large groups can be organized into many small groups that make up the whole. I learned through my experience in the cell church movement that the largest churches in the world are "cell churches," where the congregation is organized into small groups that meet in homes, restaurants, or someone's office during the week. After all, how would you get 750,000 members into one church building? Even if you had multiple services, it would be a challenge. In *Community: The Structure of Belonging*, Peter Block suggests that even large groups should break into small groups to *digest* the information that was shared from the stage.

These groups can also be called cell groups or life groups that meet on a regular basis to learn and grow together, just as every living organism is made up of cells that make life possible.

Military units are organized into squads. What is one of the most potent of the small groups in the military? The Navy SEALs, of course. Who else could pull off the elimination of Osama bin Laden, or take out the Somali pirates who boarded the U.S.-flagged ship the *Maersk Alabama* and took Captain Richard Phillips hostage?

If small, interactive groups are so effective, why don't more leaders utilize them? My hunch is that the general population hasn't really thought about it that much, hence the reason for this book and this chapter. I've studied and practiced leadership extensively for a quarter of a century, and I can't think of one single training program that has focused on the power of small groups.

Our culture has a large group mentality that's a hangover from the Industrial Revolution. When we became an industrialized culture, we became an "institutionalized" culture. We simply expect that our institutions will take care of us. When I started going to church, I didn't question the way it was done until my Tuesday night small group experience. It never crossed my mind until I saw the stark contrast between the small group meeting at which community was actually happening rather than someone just doling out information.

Our culture has a large group mentality that's a hangover from the Industrial Revolution.

Dr. Ralph Neighbour Jr. further revolutionized my thinking on this subject. In fact, the first person I remember attaching the word *community* to the small group was Ralph. I learned from him that most institutions are "program based designed," which means they build a "program" that addresses a problem. There's nothing wrong with a program, but the problem is that programs don't solve problems. People do.

Yes, information is important. Yes, inspiration is important. Yes, programs can be effective, but when you have inspiration and information without interaction that causes people to dig deep into their souls and search their hearts, you don't get maximum implementation. And you certainly don't get community.

Even when leaders become aware of the power of the POD, the vulnerability and close proximity of the small group makes their palms sweat. Sitting around a boardroom table at a client's office a few years ago, the owner of the company invited the team to let him know how they truly felt about his leadership effectiveness. It was not pretty. They scorched the man. And frankly, he deserved it because he was an absolute control freak and micromanaged everything that happened in that company. But the bigger point is how he handled the feedback he got from his team. This small group meeting at the boardroom table was his opportunity to humble himself and seek to understand why his team members felt the way they did. But he didn't. Instead, he defended himself and got angry. For the rest of the day and throughout dinner, all I heard from the man was how his employees were *wrong*. Sadly, that man still has the same culture he had before that meeting. Many leaders are afraid to be vulnerable. They are afraid of the truth. But the truth will set you free to build true community.

It seems like no matter what kind of meeting it is, we have to have a "speaker." As a professional speaker, I'm grateful for that, but why can't we have less information and more interaction?

More and more, we're going to a so-called *online community* to solve our problems for us. Going to an online community for advice from strangers seems ironic to me since we are more skeptical of others than ever. Is it possible that people go online to get information without having to actually *follow* the advice? Is the appeal of an online community the disdain for accountability? Or is it so we can avoid interacting with real people altogether?

Along with the advice you get from an online community may come insults from people you don't even know. People who don't even use their real name on their social media profile. I personally love interacting on social media because I can network with people, support people, and encourage them, but it is disconcerting to witness cyberbullies who hide behind their screen name.

Growth PODS help you connect in a very powerful way. The best kinds of PODS are face-to-face PODS, but if that isn't possible, the next best solution is videoconferencing, where at least you can see who you're talking to. Facial expressions and body language speak loudly. Even though this process is very powerful, even online, there is no substitute for in-person interaction.

The Power of the POD

PODS work because they create engagement. The entire premise of this book has been about engagement. The way the POD meeting is designed creates mandatory sharing. No one is exempt from sharing in a POD, but it is also designed to create ample space for those who haven't totally committed to the idea of engaging in such close quarters as a POD. Over time, the support, encouragement, and accountability should pull any willing person into a sense of belonging. If not, you'll have the opportunity to find out why the person doesn't want to connect, which will help you identify his or her concerns.

Here's why PODS are so powerful when they are properly facilitated:

1. **Accountability.** Participants commit to implement the things they said they wanted to accomplish. After all, who wants to show up to a group and admit he or she didn't do what he or she was supposed to do? No one.

2. **Feedback.** Participants receive input from others that will help them succeed. They get congratulations when they succeed. If they fall short, they get the support, encouragement, and accountability to keep trying.

3. **The power of discovery.** The biggest advantage of a POD (properly facilitated) is that the participants *discover* how they need to change instead of someone *telling* them what to do. When people discover something on their own, they tend to take ownership for the idea.

4. **Character growth.** Over time, when the POD is properly facilitated, POD members grow as people. Values are challenged, changed, or validated, and each person has the opportunity to grow into the person he or she needs to be.

5. **Community.** Of course community is the ultimate benefit and what this entire book is all about. Over time, when the POD is properly facilitated, a sense of belonging is created among the participants and community can eventually be realized.

6. **Multiplication.** One of the little-known benefits of PODS is the opportunity for growth and expansion. As I mentioned earlier, PODS are the building blocks for organizing large groups of people. Once you build your first POD, you'll then be able multiply that POD by developing your next POD facilitator for your second POD. Then you'll duplicate that process over and over again. Find out more at www.HowardPartridge.com/PODS.

7. **Filters.** A common lament I hear from business owners and managers is "I can't tell you how many times I told them [their employees] the same thing over and over again!" As a leader, how do you know if you're getting through to people? Of course you can look at outcomes, but isn't that a little late? Instead, we want to get regular feedback. Understanding the growth process is very important.

    There are many reasons people don't do what you want them to do, but one simple explanation is you didn't communicate well. Dr. Ralph Neighbour Jr. taught me early on we all have our own mental filters that we pass information through There are six filters people go through before they adopt a new value.

    His insight is that it takes "six to stick." As you move through your journey from wherever you are now to true community, you'll want to know about the six filters that Dr. Neighbour shares in his book *Christ's Basic Bodies.*

- Unaware. You are unaware of the value, idea, or concept.

- Aware. You become aware of the importance of the idea, concept, or value.

- Willing to change. You make a decision that you want to change. This is a big step because it involves facing the fears we spoke of earlier in the book.

- Intentional focus. Once you've made a decision and you've decided to make this value a priority, you begin to focus on it. But since we are creatures of habit, it's easy to fail at this level.

- Commitment. At this level the value is somewhat habitual. Most often you succeed, but if a big crisis comes, the perfect storm, so to speak, you'll get off track. But at this level, it really takes a lot to push you off course.

- Character. This is the ultimate level. You have truly changed. You've developed habits, and your values have actually changed.

Remember the character mirror of accountability? Regularly scheduled PODS will help you and your community members stay focused and accountable for better outcomes personally and professionally.

The Precedence for the POD

The Junto, also known as the Leather Apron Club, was a club for mutual improvement established in 1727 by Benjamin Franklin in Philadelphia. The Junto's purpose was to debate questions of morals, politics, and natural philosophy and to exchange knowledge of business affairs. It was also a charitable organization and created a subscription public library consisting of the members' own books.

Evangelist John Wesley sparked a revival in England with his small group methods. From D. Michael Henderson's book *John Wesley's Class Meetings: A Model for Making Disciples*: "The heart of this revolutionary system was a cell group of six to eight people. . . . They met weekly to give an account for their personal spiritual growth, according to the rules and following the procedures which Wesley had carefully crafted. The class meeting proved to be such an effective tool for radical personal change that it can be acknowledge as the pivotal element of the Methodist movement." This movement became what we know today as the Methodist Church.

Jeff Sutherland, in his book *Scrum: The Art of Doing Twice the Work in Half the Time*, shares the almost unbelievable results of impossible tasks being accomplished in a fraction of the time by utilizing small groups.

Leadership expert John C. Maxwell, in collaboration with Jerry Anderson, is using a small group system called RoundTables that is transforming values in South America.

Jerry Wiles is leading a movement in worldwide missions by using a revolutionary method called Orality. Here's how he describes it:

> The Orality Phenomenon is a significant development that is changing the ways people are thinking about learning, communications and behavior change. Recent studies show that the majority (more than 70%) of the people in the world are Oral Learners, by necessity or by preference. The concepts, principles and practices of Orality are changing the face of the church and mission world, but also the business world, especially as they relate to cross-cultural, international and reproducible methods and

strategies. The global marketplace is progressively becoming more complex and diverse, and therefore making the importance of understanding Orality concepts a critical area. . . .

Not only are Orality Methods effective in the bush in West Africa, they are also powerful tools in the board rooms of corporate America, and even in college and university class rooms in the modern Western World. Understanding Orality concepts and principles is very significant in terms of communicating the gospel and making disciples in every segment of society. The business world, of course, is a major part of where people live and work. Business leaders are finding orality and storytelling methods useful in area such as improving relationships and community, team building, business development, and corporate culture. A better understanding of Orality methods and strategies can also improve sales and marketing effectiveness, but also enhance efforts of any kind of communication and training at every level. . . . The newly formed Orality in Business Network is providing some additional avenues for expanding the movement.

Learn more at www.orality.net.

Blogger Janet Choi writes in her post "Cells, Pods, and Squads: The Future of Organizations Is Small" on the I Done This blog (May 1, 2014):

Think small and you will achieve big things. That's the Yoda-esque, counterintuitive philosophy that nets Finnish game company Supercell revenues of millions of dollars *a day*.

So really, how do you build a billion-dollar business by thinking small?

One key is the company's super cell organizational model. Autonomous small teams, or "cells," of four to six people position the company to be nimble and innovative. Similar modules—call them squads, pods, cells, startups within startups—are the basic components in many other nimble, growing companies, including Spotify and Automattic. The future, as Dave Gray argues in *The Connected Company*, is podular.

What is a connected company? According to The Connected Company website (connectedco.com), "Connected companies are learning organizations, with a culture of experimentation and fast feedback. How do they work? Connected companies are made up of small, semi-autonomous teams, connected by a shared purpose and a common platform that helps them coordinate joint action. What does this mean for leaders? Leaders must get used to less control and creating an environment of clarity, trust, and common purpose."

Growth PODS bring all three keys of building community—support, encouragement, and accountability, and the previous five steps into one simple structure that will not only help your company be more productive but, more important, help your team build community. PODS are the building blocks for expanding a sense of belonging, then a sense of community, and eventually the ultimate goal of true community.

In a lunch meeting with my mentor, the wisest man I know, he warned me that PODS must be experienced, not taught, so be sure to download the POD outlines at the end of this chapter.

The Procedure of the POD

The most important thing to keep in mind when facilitating a small group is that you are *facilitating*, not teaching! In fact, if you want to be a phenomenal leader and coach, stop telling people what to do and ask more questions!

If you want to be a phenomenal leader and coach,
stop telling people what to do and ask more questions!

Questions engage people. Sure, there's a time—even in a POD—when people are learning—and you may even teach, but there's even more time dedicated to the interactive parts of the POD.

Facilitating includes listening and allowing participants to interact and helping them discover the concepts themselves so they can own them. Facilitating is leading without teaching.

A POD must be at least 3 people and not more than 12. Community happens most completely in a group of 12 or less, and ideally 7 to 9, depending on the purpose of the POD and the amount of time allotted.

The time allotted for a POD depends on the purpose. For example, a daily check-in POD might be only 15 minutes, whereas a weekly department POD or coaching POD may be an hour. A weekly team POD might go 90 minutes. Don't go over 90 minutes in a POD, and encourage people not to take a break during the POD.

The Practice of the POD

A POD can be used to share information, to simply build relationships, or to complete a specific task. To learn and practice the POD, start with your two closest, most trusted team members. This is your leadership team—your inner circle—your guiding team.

Next, you'll want to determine a place to meet. One benefit of a POD is that you don't need a meeting room. It can be held at a restaurant, in someone's office, or at a conference table. It can even be held outside in a park or on the beach.

The next thing is the time and day to meet. If it's a daily POD, select the time and encourage everyone to be there on time. Do not wait for people who are late. If you do that, you will inadvertently train others to be late. Most PODS will have a weekly rhythm, so make sure you meet on the same day and at the same time every week so participants can put it into their routine.

Make sure you meet in a circle! You'll find that some people are uncomfortable in a POD setting, yet vulnerability is necessary for POD participation. Although the reason you want to do a POD is to build a sense of community, you'll likely have some resistance at some point even if you don't have it in your initial POD. Don't be surprised. People are not used to being vulnerable, and that is exactly the problem. A POD is a safe place to share as everything is kept confidential.

You may find someone who wants to sit on the outside of the circle, or wants to stand, or finds a way to create some kind of barrier between himself or herself and the group. This is a surefire indicator that this person is uncomfortable in this setting. Be sensitive to this and maybe have a one-on-one meeting with that person later in private to discuss why he or she feels that way. However, you cannot operate a POD with someone outside the circle, so ask everyone to sit in the circle with the group.

Ask participants to turn off all technology during the POD. A POD is about engagement. The purpose of the POD is to connect, and the power of the POD comes from the engagement that takes place. Texting or checking e-mail is not allowed during a POD, and computers are banned as well.

If your POD requires taking notes and people want to take notes on a device, ask them to either take notes by hand to enter later, or to put the device on airplane mode.

Some PODS will require more information than others. Should you decide to use PODS in a team meeting in which people need to refer to notes or documents or take a lot of notes, you will need more tech involved.

Regardless of the type of leading you are doing, *less is more*. Share less information to get more implementation. As Jerry Wiles teaches about oral learning methods, the goal is duplication of the material— that is, someone should be able to leave the group and effectively share what was learned. That certainly isn't the case in most information-laden meetings. The Orality Network's mantra is "Learn a little, practice a lot, implement immediately." Liz Wiseman, author of *Multipliers: How the Best Leaders Make Everyone Smarter*, encourages leaders to "play fewer chips." In other words, we would rather have maximum implementation of a little than share a lot of information that never gets implemented.

Humans have a limited amount of information they can digest at one time. Information overload is a major culprit in disengagement. In your POD, focus only on the wildly important. Trim down to the most important information and you'll get better implementation.

Information overload is a major culprit in disengagement.

All POD participants agree to keep everything in the POD confidential unless the subject matter is intended to be shared with others. Since some PODS are highly personal, it is important for everyone to agree to confidentiality in advance.

The length of a POD can vary, but typically it will be from 60 to 90 minutes. The amount of time dedicated to the Information and Interaction parts of the POD will vary with the overall time frame of the POD.

Always start on time and end on time. Waiting for people to arrive to start your POD penalizes those who are on time, and it trains those who are on time to be late. Ending a POD late demonstrates disrespect. The purpose and power of a POD is that it fosters a sense of community. Ending late can affect this purpose.

Keep in mind that when you are facilitating a POD, you are not a teacher or trainer, and you don't have to even have a title or position to lead a POD. Anyone can lead a POD, especially if the information part is preplanned and preprinted so the facilitator can simply read the information. A POD leader must simply facilitate.

Each of the five parts of a POD begins with the letter *I*. The five I's of a POD are:

1. **Icebreaker.** Engage each and every participant.

2. **Information.** Share relevant information.

3. **Interaction.** Facilitate a discussion around the information.

4. **Implementation.** Request an action item from each participant based on the information discussed.

5. **Inspiration.** Close with something inspirational.

Opening the POD: The Icebreaker

Welcome the group by thanking them for coming. Share why the group has come together. Then begin with the Icebreaker question.

The purpose of the Icebreaker is to engage the audience. Some personality profiles are less likely to open up, so the Icebreaker helps reserved types share, and it also keeps the outgoing type from dominating the meeting as each Icebreaker answer is less than 60 seconds long.

The Icebreaker question should be positive, since all of your meetings should start on a positive note. You'll want a question that can be answered in 60 seconds or less, but avoid questions that can be answered with one word such as *yes*, *no*, or *good*. See the Practice PODS referenced at the end of this chapter for examples.

Answering the Icebreaker question is mandatory for every participant. The POD facilitator answers first to model the answer, then it moves clockwise around the circle from there. Remember that your participants probably will follow your pattern, so make sure your answer is a good model to follow. Ensure that your answer is 60 seconds or less. As the facilitator you are modeling the time frame as well.

Ensure that each person stays within the time limit. You may want to assign a timekeeper to keep the group on track, especially if you have a lot of outgoing people in your group. Of course, this becomes more important as your group grows. For now, you'll just start with a group of three.

It is important that there be no discussion during the Icebreaker. Many times when someone shares an answer to the Icebreaker question, it triggers a thought in someone else's mind, and that person has the urge to share the thought. Encourage participants that there will be ample time to share during the Interaction time and that the purpose of the Icebreaker is for each person to engage, not to generate a discussion yet. However, the Icebreaker should be fun and not cold or dry. Therefore, comments of affirmation are encouraged from the facilitator. Since you are running the group, it is appropriate for you to make a short comment or simply compliment each person as you go around the circle.

Once the person immediately to your right has answered the Icebreaker, move to Information.

Information

The second *I* is about the Information that needs to be shared with the group. This is the learning segment that includes the information your group needs to know on this particular occasion. For example, if you're using a POD for your team meeting, the information will most likely be around the progress of the projects that the team is working on. For example, in *Scrum*, author Jeff Sutherland outlines the Scrum meeting, in which the product owner shares the progress of the project the group is working on.

If it is a Learning POD in which the group is learning a specific subject, the group will take in the next block of information required. For example, I have a weekly leadership POD in which I teach a group of my coaching members leadership concepts. Sometimes we go through specific training programs in which there is a set of teaching materials that we follow. Other times, I simply teach what I'm learning, or a guest speaker will share.

The information can be shared in any way the facilitator deems best. Presentation slides can be used, stories can be told, a video can be played, or participants can read together the way you'll do in your Practice POD. Any teaching method can be used, and it doesn't have to be done by the facilitator. Any participant in the group or even an outside speaker can bring the Information piece. How you deliver information will depend on what you are teaching and the skill level of the person presenting the information.

The power of the POD comes in the Interaction part that comes after the Information session. Remember that the power of discovery is the key to a POD. Powerful, life-changing concepts are usually not *taught*, they are *caught*. Facilitating the discussion after the Information is when the power of discovery happens. The purpose of the Information segment is to provide *direction* to the discussion that comes afterward.

The Information session will be 15 to 30 minutes depending on the length and size of the POD.

A 60-minute POD will look like this:

Icebreaker: 10 to 15 minutes depending on the size of the group

Information: 15 minutes

Interaction: 15 minutes

Implementation: 10 to 15 minutes depending on the size of the group

Inspiration: 5 minutes or less

A 90-minute POD simply has more Information and Interaction time:

Icebreaker: 10 to 15 minutes depending on the size of the group

Information: 30 minutes

Interaction: 30 minutes

Implementation: 10 to 15 minutes depending on the size of the group

Inspiration: 5 minutes or less

It's preferable to switch back and forth between Information and Interaction over a one-hour period to keep everyone engaged.

Interaction

The purpose of the Interaction segment is to generate a discussion around the information that was shared. The Interaction segment is voluntary. Everyone does not have to answer the questions, although it would be a pretty boring POD if no one did. Keep in mind that you probably don't have enough time for everyone to share his or her response to every question that is asked in the Interaction segment, so don't go around the circle the way you did with the Icebreaker. However, you definitely want people to interact, because this is where the magic happens! That is, *if* you do a good job facilitating.

Effective facilitating is a skill that takes time and training. Facilitating doesn't come naturally. You'll want to connect with our community to learn how to become a seasoned POD facilitator. There are some common challenges with facilitating. For example, what do you do if everyone goes silent? How to do you create the right discussion questions? These are all legitimate and important questions. Since the power of discovery happens in this segment, it's extremely important to get it right.

The first and most important thing to keep in mind during this segment is that you are *done* teaching! The Information segment is over. Resist the temptation to teach. In fact, resist making a statement at all. Tap into the power of the question instead.

Phenomenal leaders ask great questions. Asking good questions is key to coaching, and as a leader, you are a coach. In fact, if you can't coach well, you can't lead well. Make it your goal to become a good coach rather than a good teacher. A good coach asks good questions.

Phenomenal leaders ask great questions.

Why are questions so important? Isn't it because good questions engage people? Isn't it because good questions also make people think? Isn't it true that people will catch or discover more when you ask them questions rather than telling them what to do? Have you heard that selling isn't telling? Isn't it true that when you're holding a POD, you're *selling* a concept or idea? What happens when you give too much information? Is it possible that information overload is more likely to overwhelm people, making it likely they will implement less if anything at all? Does it make sense that overloading people with too much information can paralyze them with fear? Have you heard of the "paralysis of analysis"? Did you notice that this entire paragraph doesn't have a single statement but is made up entirely of questions? How will asking better questions help you? Can you see how questions engage and empower the participants of your POD?

So, what does a good question look like? Good questions start with *what*, *how*, and *why*:

> "What was something you got out of the information that was shared?"

> "How are you planning on using the information that was shared?"

> "Why is that important to you?"

Can you see how others in your POD can discover things for themselves as someone else answers the questions?

Make sure you resist the urge to answer the question or to move too quickly to the next question! Depending on the group dynamics, you may or may not have a lot of talkers. In some PODS, you have so much interaction that it's hard to bring it to a close. In other situations, you have a quiet, reserved group. A good facilitator has to learn how to handle these situations.

If you have a quiet group and you aren't getting the interaction you want, ask the group members to share what they are thinking about. Again, if your group consists of more reserved personalities, you may have this occur.

The other reasons participants may not interact at a high level is that they don't know one another well enough to open up, or there may be trust issues or conflict among the team members. Although, the POD is a powerful setting for growth and change, it may be slow getting interaction. That's okay. You cannot force genuine relationships. They grow over time.

Implementation

Many meetings end with no call to action. Many times people leave a meeting wondering, "What did we decide to do?" In the Implementation segment of the POD, each participant will share an action step he or she plans to take as a result of the POD meeting. In this step it is mandatory for each person to share. Depending on time, you can allow up to 60 seconds for a response or as little as 15 seconds for each person to make a quick statement.

The purpose of this step is to get the participants to verbalize an action step. Verbalizing an action step garners more implementation from participants, and it will also reveal what they have discovered.

Inspiration

The final step in the POD is to end with something highly encouraging. It could be a simple quote, a story, a video, or a quick exercise. Choose something uplifting that relates to the subject matter of the POD. For example, if you were having a POD with your leadership team around vision, you could quote Helen Keller. Keller was reportedly asked, "What could be worse than being blind?" Her response: "The only thing worse than being blind is having sight with no vision."

The POD facilitator does not have to be the one to do the Inspiration part. Someone else in the group can do it. If you do have someone else do the Inspiration part, make sure you know what they are going to share or you have a high level of trust and confidence in the person sharing. The last thing you want to do is end your POD on a questionable note.

An simple, easy way to do this is to simply share your most meaningful takeaway from the POD. In fact, that's what we will do in the Practice PODS below.

The Practice of the POD

I was having lunch with my early mentor Bill Beckham, who taught me how to facilitate cell groups, and he urged me to have you practice a POD, because PODS must be experienced to really understand them.

Therefore, I've created 12 simple PODS around the content of this book. If you do a weekly POD, this outline creates a perfect 90-day process in which you can get your core leadership team together and discuss the merits of building community and absorb the content of this book in the context of a POD.

To get started, you'll need to invite some participants. If you have a leadership team or you have people selected to be part of your guiding team, invite them to the POD. If you don't have a leadership team but you want to do a POD around this book, invite some fellow leaders to join you.

They will need a copy of this book, so ensure that everyone in your group has a copy before you start your practice POD. Share the purpose of the POD with them—that you want to practice a new format of meeting together that has the potential for greater understanding, ownership, and implementation than traditional meeting structures. Share that you want them to experience a POD first, before you use PODS in other areas of your company. Download the POD outline for each chapter and get facilitating tips at http://www.howardpartridge.com/PODS.

DEVELOP YOUR COMMUNITY SYSTEMS

Every tribe and every community has its unique ways of doing things. In other words, all of them have systems. Installing systems in your business will help you live out the essence of community but also comes with additional benefits, as you'll see in this chapter.

Business owners and leaders often feel overwhelmed because they have to be involved in every aspect of the business. You may even feel like a slave to your business or job. As one leader put it, "I feel like I'm at the bottom of a giant slide, and all the problems just flow right down onto my desk."

As a business owner, I know what that's like. I was a slave to my business before I learned to lead, attract the right people, and build systems in my business. I also know what it's like to own a predictable, profitable, turnkey operation—a business that operates without my daily involvement.

I've found that to be phenomenally successful, every organization needs three things:

1. **Phenomenal leadership.** Everything rises or falls on leadership.

2. **Phenomenal people.** If you don't hire the right people, nothing else works. Phenomenal leadership helps you attract phenomenal people.

3. **Phenomenal systems.** Even the best talent needs a track to run on.

My good friend David Frey uses this acronym for SYSTEM:

Save

Yourself

Time

Energy

Money

When your team members know what to do, how to do it, and why they are doing it, less time, energy, and money are required to make it happen. It always takes more time, energy, and money to rethink and re-create something than it does simply to follow a procedure.

You may have seen the numbers test that some seminar presenters use. It has a collection of numbers that are seemingly randomly thrown onto the paper. As a participant, you have to find the numbers in order as fast as you can. After the timer goes off, the facilitator reveals that the numbers are grouped into quadrants on the page. Once you know the *system* of the numbers, you can find them much more easily and faster with less energy. In the same way, when you have systems in place, your team is empowered and you don't have to make all the decisions, therefore saving yourself time, energy, and money.

Without systems companies may grow in revenue but suffer in profits.

Without systems you cannot lead effectively. Systems are communication tools.

Without systems your team members won't perform at their highest level.

Without systems your service experience won't be as predictable.

Without systems the behavior of your team members won't be as predictable.

Systems keep the leader focused as well. All too often, leaders who know where they can fudge by circumventing the system do it at the risk of influencing other team members to do the same. The problem is that team members may not have the experience you have as the owner or leader.

Many years ago, I went on an on-site consultation for one of my companies. I just assumed the prospect wasn't going to buy, so I never entered any information on the proposal into the computer. As you can probably guess, the prospect did call. Getting caught short-circuiting the system wasn't the best example I could have made for my team member who took the inbound call, to say the least.

If you ever want to sell your business, you have to understand that potential buyers won't be looking for an overwhelming job where they have to make all the decisions. They will want a set of keys to a predictable, profitable turnkey operation.

I love the story of Somebody, Everybody, and Nobody (drawn from a poem on responsibility by Charles Osgood):

> Somebody was asked to do something that was Everybody's job.
> Everybody thought Somebody was going to do it, but Nobody did

it. When Nobody did it, Everybody asked why Somebody didn't do it. Somebody said it was Everybody's job. Everybody said it was Nobody's job, therefore Nobody did it.

A system is simply a group of working parts that make up the whole. The Five P's of Building Your Community System are:

1. **Purpose.** Why your community exists.

2. **Positions.** The roles of the team members.

3. **PRDs (Performance Results Descriptions).** What each team member is responsible for.

4. **Policies.** The rules of the game.

5. **Procedures.** The team playbook.

The First P: Purpose

We've talked a lot about vision throughout this book, and this is where you get to actually identify it. Your vision is your mission, values, and purpose (MVP), and of course your organization will have goals as well. As a business, you'll have many goals ranging from revenues and profits to customer service to production goals. Nonprofits might have donor goals, outreach goals, or any number of outcome goals. But more important than individual goals as it relates to community is your purpose.

Author Simon Sinek's sensational TED Talk video *Start with Why* is one of the most watched TED Talks in existence. The premise of *Start with Why* is that most companies are "what" companies that say, "This is what we *do*," and some are even "how" companies, which differentiates them to some degree, but "why" companies inspire others.

The "why" of your organization is its purpose. Why does your organization exist? What difference does it make in the world? What void would exist if your company or organization didn't exist?

For example, one of the companies I own is a service company that cares for high-end oriental rugs and natural stone floors for some of Houston's most prominent citizens, celebrities, and world leaders—names you would recognize. Our purpose is to "protect our clients from unethical service companies." Many in-home service companies don't show up on time, they don't do background checks, and they don't always tell the truth.

Our purpose is to protect our community from that scenario by being the "knights in shining armor." That's our *why*. That's our purpose. We also have a mission statement and five values.

Your Mission

Your mission is *what* you do every day. Our mission at that company is "to provide the most outstanding service experience ever." That's what we do every day. I understand that some companies view mission the way I view goals, and that's okay. If you define your words a little differently, at least you're communicating your direction to your team (and your clients, as we'll see in the next chapter).

Our mission at my coaching company Phenomenal Products is "to help small business owners stop being a slave to their business." The mission statement of our Inner Circle Coaching Community is "to create the most phenomenal community experience ever." What we know is that the number one reason organizations don't grow or do as well as they could is something I call FTI (Failure to Implement).

When our members engage in a community experience, they are much more likely to implement because they have the support, encouragement, and accountability that come from belonging to a community.

Your Values

Your values are *who* you are as a company, or at least who you want to become as a company. Patrick Lencioni talks about *aspirational* values (who you want to become) and *actual* values (who you actually are). As leaders, we must continually communicate our aspirational values and identify the gaps between aspirational and actual.

Your values might be integrity, loyalty, honesty, or things of that nature. Have no more than three to five core values because you want your team members to be able to recite them and to flesh out what they mean in everyday community life.

Our five values in both of my main companies are:

1. **Reputation.** My good friend Dr. Joseph A. Michelli, who is an international branding expert and a number one *New York Times* bestselling author, describes a brand as "what people say about you when you're not around." We value our reputation, so we protect and promote it at every turn.

2. **Experience.** This is how long you've been doing what you do, or the experience you have in your field. This is very important in most professions unless the business is a new concept. In that case, one of your values would speak to innovation rather than experience. In our case, we value experience and pass it on to our clients. The fact that I've been a business owner myself for 33 years and have been helping small business owners worldwide for two decades is a strong statement of experience, for example.

3. **Training.** Training builds confidence. You cannot consistently provide the most outstanding service experience or a phenomenal community experience if your team isn't

trained properly. We value training. Therefore, we invest in training at a very high level.

4. **Systems.** You can't provide a consistent experience without systems. We value systems, and therefore we're always talking about how we can make things run more smoothly. Systems make everyday community life more predictable.

5. **Guarantee (commitment or warranty).** If you can offer a 100 percent money-back guarantee on your product or service, by all means do it. The way you handle your guarantee will directly affect your reputation, so by all means put a high value on your guarantee. If you're in an industry in which you cannot legally offer a money-back guarantee (such as in financial services or real estate), you may want to use the word *commitment* or *warranty*.

For example, a home builder obviously can't give people's money back if they aren't happy with their house, but that builder can commit to a warranty. My wife and I have been blessed to build two dream homes, one in Texas and one in Florida. In both cases, our builders were phenomenal. Long after the warranties had run out on our Houston home, when anything needed to be fixed, the builder dispatched someone right away to fix the problem.

Your Purpose

Again, your purpose is your *why*. Our purpose statement at Phenomenal Products is "To help our clients have more L.I.F.E." My acronym for L.I.F.E. is Living In Freedom Every day. There's no freedom in being broke and in debt. There's no freedom in having a disengaged team or unhappy clients. But we can all live in freedom in our minds and hearts if we know we are becoming the person we are supposed to be and we are doing the things we know to do.

The biggest reason you want to have a meaningful purpose is to connect what each of your team members does every day to the difference it makes in your customer's life. Inspiration happens when your team members understand *why* they are doing what they are doing, and how it makes a difference in the lives of their customers.

The Second P: Positions

The next step is to identify your team positions. Not just the titles but their function as well. Over the last three decades of running my own companies and the last two decades of helping other business owners, professionals, and nonprofits become more successful, I've identified five systems of a business and three levels of leadership.

The five systems are:

1. **Leadership.** Communicating the vision.

2. **Marketing.** Attracting prospects.

3. **Sales.** Converting prospects into customers.

4. **Operations.** Delivering the experience.

5. **Administration.** Tracking the stats.

The three levels of leadership are:

1. **Directing.** Setting the vision.

2. **Managing.** Supervising the actions.

3. **Implementing.** Doing the work.

Keeping in mind that "leadership is influence," leadership needs to happen at every level in the organization. Everyone is a leader because everyone has influence on another person in the company. This is the reason a culture of community is so important. Each and every team member has the opportunity to influence another team member, client, or vendor positively or negatively.

When you put it all together, the functional organizational chart would look like Figure 10.1.

ORGANIZATIONAL CHART				
LEADERSHIP	MARKETING	SALES	OPERATIONS	ADMINISTRATION
Directing (Planning)				
Managing (Supervising)				
Implementing (Doing)				

Figure 10.1   Organizational Chart

When you fill this chart in, each of your team members will be able to see where he or she fits and the importance of his or her position on the team. It also helps team members see what everyone else does, which helps eliminate the feeling that others' work isn't as important as theirs.

The Third P: PRDs

A Performance Results Description (PRD), similar to a job description, outlines the results that are required for that position and the performance that is expected to achieve the results. An example might be a sales goal (result) and the number of calls to be made in a day (performance) to reach that goal.

The Fourth P: Policies

Every game has boundaries and rules of the game. In your organization, your employee handbook would be a good example of a set of policies, but you also want to have policies attached to the PRD. For example, if the bookkeeper's responsibility is to make daily bank deposits, you would have a policy of when those deposits are to be made.

The Fifth P: Procedures

Procedures are the "how to" of the business. For each major task, outline the steps or the script for each one. Staying with the bookkeeper analogy, you would outline the step-by-step procedures on *how* the deposit is done.

It will take time to put all of this together, and you'll need the support of your team (another reason for creating community), but when you systematize your organization, your community will be able to deliver the community experience *consistently*, which is what we'll cover in the next chapter.

CREATE YOUR COMMUNITY BRAND EXPERIENCE

CHAPTER 11

The final phase of this journey is extending your community brand experience to your customers, clients, guests, patients, donors, or members. When your clients feel that they belong to your community, they will be more loyal, and they will refer you more. What sets a company apart more than anything else is the customer experience. And at the top of the food chain of experiences is a community brand experience. What is that exactly?

First off, an experience is an emotional journey. Think of theater, for example. When I ask my seminar audiences what theater is, the typical response is "entertainment." "What is entertainment?" I press. Entertainment is a presentation designed to make you feel a certain way. The best presentations make you *feel* something at a designated time.

If a theater production, a movie, or any kind of presentation flops, it's usually because it didn't stir emotion. Everyone knows that steely data, no matter how accurate it is, doesn't inspire. An experience properly created invokes emotion that in turn inspires people.

Some Examples

This section highlights some companies that have created a positive community brand experience.

Starbucks

A community brand experience is one in which your clients feel like they belong to your brand. Starbucks has done an amazing job with this. In fact, the creation of Starbucks as we know it today came from a "community epiphany" Howard Schultz had in Milan, Italy. At the time he was the national marketing director for Starbucks—a small Seattle-based company that sold coffee beans to coffee enthusiasts. At that time, Starbucks didn't offer coffee drinks.

Howard Schultz's epiphany came as he tasted an espresso in a corner espresso bar amidst the sun-drenched Italian architecture. He realized that community was happening right before his eyes. Neighbors met for a latte. Couples romanced over a cappuccino, and businessmen negotiated over an espresso. As they came and went on their Vespas, Howard Schultz imagined re-creating that community experience back in Seattle.

The owners of Starbucks wouldn't have it. The tale is told in a book Howard wrote called *Pour Your Heart Into It: How Starbucks Built a Company One Cup at a Time*. He left the company and started his own little chain of espresso bars called *Il Giornale* (named after a Milanese newspaper). Schultz later bought Starbucks and created one of the greatest examples of a community brand experience ever.

However, creating the experience and maintaining the experience while experiencing massive growth is always a challenge. New leadership and eventually a recession brought the real test. In *Onward: How Starbucks Fought for Its Life Without Losing Its Soul*, Howard Schultz explains how the brand experience was diluted. One of the seemingly innocent changes that were made during that time period were new espresso machines that were more accurate (therefore saving time and money) but did not create the aroma the more manual machines did. Starbucks had overlooked the fact that part of the experience was the pulling of the espresso and the permeating smell of coffee when customers walked into the store. Howard Schultz stepped back in and put the company back on track.

Community brands tend to permeate customers' lives in ways that become a part of their personal identity. As a demonstration of how this can happen, I'll share something personal. I talk about Starbucks a lot in my talks, and I happen to frequent Starbucks locations around the world quite often, and I buy a lot of its coffee beans.

I don't recall how it first began, but I started collecting Starbucks mugs from different cities and countries. These beautiful mugs have the name of the city, state, or country with artwork depicting the landscape, architecture, or icons of that area. When I published my first book, I promoted on social media that I would trade a signed copy of my book for a Starbucks mug that I did not yet own. I posted a list of cups I had at the time, and mugs began to show up at my office.

Around that same time, I did a webcast for Ziglar with Tom Ziglar. He had just returned from Ireland and presented me with a mug on the air. We ended up using that video as a promotional tool for the next couple of years. As a result, I *still* get Starbucks mugs shipped to me. I have over 140 mugs at this time.

Southwest Airlines

Another great example of a company that creates phenomenal experiences for its customers is Southwest Airlines. In fact, Southwest is where fun and LUV are part of the everyday experience. LUV is Southwest Airlines' stock symbol. With heartwarming public announcements recognizing active military personnel on board, a fiftieth anniversary, or someone's very first flight, Southwest spreads the LUV daily. And Southwest is known for its humorous safety announcements, singing, and cracking jokes. On a recent flight, just before landing, a flight attendant in the front began singing the *Final Destination* script. When she finished, the flight attendant in the back picked up her microphone and announced that there was a passenger on board who was 90 years old and it was his first flight. Everyone clapped. She then encouraged everyone to congratulate the man with this request: "When you get off the plane, please congratulate the captain" (insinuating that the captain flying the aircraft was 90 and it was his first flight, if you didn't get that). Everyone loved it.

I travel Southwest often and have a habit of recognizing the flight attendants by name and encouraging them. Not only do I get better service because of it, often they will interact quite a bit with me. I might sign a book for an attendant or have a meaningful conversation about life. But some of them use it as an opportunity to have some fun. I fell asleep during the peanut handout one night and was surprised not to find any peanut packages on my tray when I woke up.

The truth is that I couldn't care less about the peanuts, but it was a great opportunity to razz the flight attendant. "Rhonda, what's the deal? I fall asleep and I don't get any peanuts? What kind of service is that?" I teased. "I'll take care of you, troublemaker" she shot back. Troublemaker? Obviously, my small talk upon boarding the plane had gotten her attention. She came back with a large cellophane bag full of peanut packages. "Here ya go," she said. I was already chuckling at the sight of the huge bag of peanuts when she tore the plastic bag open and poured the peanut packages all over my lap.

Once she finished dumping the peanut packages, she looked at me with a grin and declared, "That ought to keep you busy for a while." I howled with laughter. The next day, I was speaking to an audience of 500 people at a conference. I told the story and began to throw peanut packages out to the audience. They loved it.

The reaction of that audience showed me I was on to something. So, on the way back from D.C. that day, I told the flight attendants what had happened on my previous flight. The next thing I knew, they loaded me up with another huge bag of peanut packages. That was almost a year ago, and as of this writing I've been throwing Southwest peanuts out to audiences ever since.

There are actually several messages here, but the chief message is that by creating a Fun-LUVing experience, Southwest extended the Fun-LUVing brand to a bigger audience. Companies that create extraordinary experiences for people go viral.

The promise of this book is that when you create a sense of community among your team members and you have a solid mission, it spills over to your customers, creating loyalty and therefore resulting in higher profits. Southwest Airlines has been the most profitable airline in the sky since its inception. Of course, its team members' commitment to its values of fun and LUV aren't the only reason. It also has effective systems. Many books have been written about Southwest Airlines, so I won't rehash the story here.

Southwest Airlines' mission statement contains only 21 words and gets right to the point. In contrast, United Airlines' mission statement is 116 words and includes the term "genuine community," yet several instances in which customers have been mistreated by United have gone viral.

Everything rises and falls on leadership, and leadership is effectively communicating the vision (mission, values, and purpose). One big takeaway from this discussion is that putting "genuine community" in your mission statement and not living it out actually positions you worse than if you didn't put it in there at all. Southwest lives out its mission statement better than most companies I have seen. In fact, it calls itself "the airline with heart." Its logo is actually a heart.

Chick-fil-A

A couple of years ago I was at Chick-fil-A headquarters attending a leadership conference. At some point during the presentation, Mark Miller, vice president of high performance leadership at Chick-fil-A, sounded off: "Community is our new differentiator!" Obviously, that got my attention since I've been thinking about this subject for many years. People like Mark Miller recognize the need for this sense of community and have found ways to incorporate it into the customer experience.

The following stories from the Chick-fil-A blog *The Chicken Wire* (thechickenwire.chick-fil-a.com) demonstrate how Chick-fil-A has created an experience that builds community.

"These Adorable Pics from Daddy Daughter Date Night Will Make You Smile" highlights an annual Chick-fil-A event:

> For a few nights, every year, all over the country, something special happens at Chick-fil-A restaurants. Little girls wearing their prettiest outfits walk into dining rooms filled with flowers, holding the hands of one very special guy: daddy. . . .
>
> Jeff Rouse, owner of the Chick-fil-A at Olathe Pointe in Olathe, Kansas, started the Daddy Daughter Date Night nine years ago. Now, hundreds of Chick-fil-A restaurants nationwide are hosting their own events, each with their own unique touches—flowers on the table, red carpets, even carriage rides or live music—to create lifelong memories for families.

"All Cooped Up: How One Chick-fil-A Operator Is Redefining the Phrase" tells about the Cell Phone Coop challenge invented by a Chick-fil-A franchise owner in Suwanee, Georgia, to help families reconnect:

> Brad Williams, a father of four, . . . wanted to ensure his family stayed connected in this technological age. . . .
>
> Realizing the "no cell phone" rule worked at home, he decided to apply the same concept in his restaurant. Thus, the "Cell Phone Coop" challenge was born. . . . The restaurant places a small, square box, (a.k.a. the Coop) on each table, with a simple challenge: enjoy a meal without the distraction of cell phones and receive a free Chick-fil-A Icedream. . . . "The challenge has completely taken off," says Williams.

The 3 E's of Experience

The 3 E's of Experience outline a simple way to outline the community brand experience.

1. **Engage.** Engagement is how you interact with someone. The goal is to connect in a personal, meaningful way to get the experience off to a good start.

2. **Educate.** Education is simply helping people understand the brand so that they can make the right choices throughout the experience.

3. **Entertain.** Serve your target audience by creating experiences for them. Entertainment isn't exclusive to funny videos or theatrics but involves "going the extra mile" and serving your clients in a way that is meaningful to them, that also can grow into a relationship that feels like community.

Delivering a phenomenal community brand experience starts with leadership and should continue with marketing and throughout the sales process. You cannot expect to deliver a phenomenal community experience if you do not effectively communicate the vision of doing so (leadership), market an experience rather than a transaction, and reinforce the promise of the experience in the sales process by building a relationship. It begins with the vision being communicated and continues with effective implementation.

In reference to leadership, earlier chapters have covered what creating a meaningful community experience among your team members means.

Then in marketing, an effective experiential marketing process involves inviting your target audience to an opportunity in which they can experience the product or service, educating them on making the right choice (even if it isn't with your company), and entertaining them or serving them in some way to make the experience special and meaningful.

Apple Stores are a great example of this. The stores are beautifully designed and inviting. The devices are available to use, and someone is standing by to assist. Everything about the experience is elegantly done.

The Free Trial Offer Experience

Chick-fil-A began the trend of offering free samples in food courts across the country. To this day, Dan Cathy has a "free chicken sandwich" offer on the back of his business card. After he gave his business card to me, I couldn't wait to see the face of the wide-eyed 16-year-old in the drive-through window at my local Chick-fil-A. She was not only ecstatic to receive the card, but she gave it back to me to use again!

I call this process the free trial offer experience. I began paying attention to this way back in 1999 when Seth Godin revolutionized the thinking of marketers with his book *Permission Marketing*. Offering a free consultation, a free sample, a free service, or something that is not just a sales pitch is a great way to engage, educate, and entertain your target audience. Since then, many a marketer has caught on to this, so you have to be more meaningful and relevant than ever and figure out how to be different, but the fact is, by creating an experience for your target audience before they become customers, then continuing the experience throughout the sales and service experience, positions you to take your brand to the ultimate level, which makes clients feel like family.

In marketing, starting the engagement step with the free trial offer can be a powerful beginning of the community brand experience. When I was shopping for my first new Lexus and didn't immediately make the decision to buy, the salesperson quickly offered that I could take it home to try it out. When I shared that I couldn't make it back to the dealership the next day, he insisted that I keep the new car for the weekend. Then I said that I had to drive to Austin (from Houston) on Monday. He replied, "No problem! Keep it for the week. We'll fill it with gas for you." Why was this salesperson so adamant about me taking that vehicle home? I think you know how the story ends. I liked how the car drove. I liked how it looked in my driveway, and I liked how I felt owning it—because I bought it when the trial week was up.

But marketing is just the beginning of the experience. A company has to maintain the experience and even upgrade and elevate that experience as time goes on and as our culture changes.

Some years later, one of my cars was totaled in one of Houston's notorious floods. I called the dealership and told the salesperson I wanted the same car. Same color. Just give me the newest model. But when I walked into the dealership, a high-priced convertible seduced me. I found myself driving off with it rather than the one I had intended on taking home. It was an amazing car in many ways, but there were several things I hated about it. After owning it for only four days, I called the manager. "I don't know how to tell you this . . ." I began. "Don't worry," he calmed me down. "Just bring it back and we'll put you in whatever you want." Because of the way this was handled, I upgraded from the model I had to a more expensive model.

One of the coolest examples I've ever had with a free trial offer experience was in Panama City Beach, Florida. I wanted to learn how to fly, and after a couple of exchanges over e-mail with the two flight schools at that airport, I could already tell a lot about the two companies.

The engagement from one company was immediate and warm. The other was slow and cold. Visiting the two flight schools confirmed my feelings. One educated me on the ins and outs of the flying experience. The other fatigued me with irrelevant facts and figures.

The more positive flight school then followed up and offered me a "free discovery flight." I was delighted. When I showed up at the FBO on that crisp, sunny Florida morning, the flight instructor advised me that they would be flying me in a "special plane" (my mentioning that I might want to own my own plane one day had not escaped his notice) and "we'll be landing at Tyndall Air Force Base, then we'll drive you back." "How do we have permission to land at an Air Force base? Why are you driving me back?" I inquired, obviously confused. "You'll see," was all he would give me.

After landing the modern, leather-seated, smart-looking Cessna TTx, I realized why we were there. The company was gearing up for one of the biggest airshows in the country, and that little plane would be on display for sale. Over the next couple of hours, I had a semiprivate air show as fighter jets roared past, biplanes did barrel rolls, and paratroopers fell from the sky with streams of smoke trailing behind them.

As we walked past a lineup of Raptor fighter jets and under a huge B-2 bomber, I marveled, "You guys really know how to put on an experience for a guy, don't you?" He just smiled. I didn't take flight lessons then, but I can tell you that when I do, I will march straight over to that flight school.

The Sales Experience

When our son turned 16, my wife and I were in the market for a brand-new Honda for him. We knew exactly what car we wanted, what the pricing was, and there were no financial issues. This should have been a very simple and easy transaction. I went onto the website of a nearby dealership. The website was inviting, and it had an opt-in where I could put in my cell phone number, which I did. In less than three minutes, my cell phone rang. Impressive.

The pleasant young lady on the other end of the phone persuaded me to come in to the dealership that same day. When I arrived, I learned that she was in the "Internet marketing department" and "didn't do sales." That was fine with me except that what unfolded before me after that was the most disjointed, inept experience I've ever seen in a sales department.

I did purchase a brand-new Honda, but not from that dealership. I didn't buy the car there because they made me wait and made it a difficult experience. It took forever to show me the car, and I had to sit and wait for them to confirm the price, and they kept me waiting. The company's website engaged me and the young woman over the phone educated me, but the sales department failed to do either.

What could the dealership have done differently to gain me as a customer and to have a chance at making me part of its client community? Starting from the beginning, the salespeople could have engaged me by using my name. They could have connected with me on the reason I was buying the car. Once they learned that financing was no issue, they could even have upsold me. They could have noticed that I'm a "high D" on the DISC profile. They would have realized that my entire goal was to get in, purchase the car, and get out as fast as possible. In this particular case, it would have been better to buy the car from a robot! To entertain me, they could have made some sort of accommodations if I had to wait. A break room with coffee. WiFi. Television. Something.

And if they wanted to advance their token boldly toward a phenomenal community experience, they could have offered to deliver the car. That would have been a "WOW" experience that I would be writing about in this book rather than what I'm writing now. By going to that level of service experience, they could have learned about my home life, whether my wife or I needed a car as well, and possibly met the neighbors or generated some referrals. Maybe they would have asked good questions about my work and asked if they could come and "entertain" my staff or clients in order to get exposed to a larger audience. But they didn't.

In sales, engagement includes everything from how salespeople look, how they sound, body language, tone of voice, and the words they use to mirror communication styles. If salespeople understand the DISC Model of Human Behavior outlined in a previous chapter, they could speed up for a D (Dominant type), exchange stories with an I (Inspiring type), slow down for an S (Supportive type), and ask a C (Cautious type) lots of questions. Using a person's name is extremely important. Engaging by asking good questions is another factor. Educating prospects on making a good decision about the product or service elevates your position. Instead of being just an order taker, you're adding value to your prospect, which in turn causes the person to feel better about you and your brand. This is something the Honda salesperson could have done easily.

Make Sure the Experience You Deliver Is as Good as Your Marketing

On Thanksgiving Day of 2012, Tom Ziglar and I were texting back and forth on some minor issues revolving around a five-city seminar tour in Australia we were leaving for the next day. All of a sudden, he texted me that his dad was heading to the emergency room. I ended up going on the trip alone to do five full-day seminars in different cities in just seven days. Translation: Fly into a city, go to sleep. Bring your luggage to the seminar room the next morning and do it all over again. The only exception was a four-and-a-half hour flight each way to Perth.

During the trip, I was staying in touch with Tom to find out how Zig was doing. He continued to decline, and I continued to refresh my e-mail and check my messages before I went to sleep in the third city. I woke up in Melbourne the next morning to the news that Zig had passed away. There were 13,000 Facebook comments on Zig's page in the first 24 hours, and it was a national news story in the United States and a trending topic on Twitter.

I felt sad for the family, sad for myself, and I had to face my third audience, which was not even expecting me. The headliner for the tour was Tom Ziglar. I had to tell them that Tom wasn't there and that Zig Ziglar, the man the seminar tour was branded around, was gone. Needless to say, the emotional journey on top of the rest of the trip was merciless.

The proverbial light at the end of the tunnel was that I had scheduled four days on a beautiful island on the Great Barrier Reef. The island was stunning. The website was exquisite, and the sales process was seamless. I elected to take a helicopter to the island instead of the only other option, which was a bumpy, windy, two-hour boat ride crammed with a bunch of people.

The island itself was breathtaking, but the view of the Great Barrier Reef from the air was heart-stopping. As the copter swayed back and forth, descending onto the helipad, I halfway expected a little guy in a white suit to come running out cheering, "Da plane! Da plane!" like the familiar scene from the old TV show *Fantasy Island*. Perhaps there would be a waiter standing at attention with a tray of tropical drinks decorated with fruit and little paper umbrellas. But no. That's not what happened.

A guy shooed the few people off the aircraft, grabbed the baggage and threw it onto a cart, and herded us up to the front desk of the resort. Over the next four days, I never heard a guest being called by name. I was "Room 157." That was the extent of the engagement. If the resort staff members happened to be walking by, they made sure they didn't make eye contact with a guest, obviously so that the guest wouldn't ask them a question.

The resort owners offered some educational sessions on the reef and the birds in the sanctuary, but the entertainment factor had totally escaped them. What could they have done differently in this case? Well, a volume of books could be written on this one subject alone, but there was one simple thing they could have done that would have made all the difference in the world.

They could have simply connected to their guests to find out why they were on the island and what they were looking forward to and made an effort to ensure that experience took place. In my case, simply learning about what I had experienced over the previous few days would have armed them with all the ammunition they needed to wow my socks off. A note, even if it was written on *leaf*, would probably be among some of my most sentimental possessions to this day, considering the circumstances.

The point of this story is that the resort's marketing was good. Its sales process was seamless. But it absolutely blew it on the delivery. And because of that, the resort owners are getting negative reviews instead of positive referrals, when they had the chance to begin a long-lasting relationship with someone who could have been pointing his audience toward that island resort by name over the last five years.

Turn Customers into Phenomenal Lifetime Community Members

The goal is to turn customers into phenomenal lifetime community members. This requires you to think about the process from customers' first interaction with your company. I call it the Client Ascension Model—moving people from "suspect" to phenomenal lifetime community member.

Suspect. A suspect is someone who fits your target market profile but has not taken any interest in your company yet.

Prospect. A prospect is someone who has shown interest by responding to an invitation to find out more. Maybe the person opted in to your website, gave you his or her business card, or called your company. You can intentionally move people from suspect to prospect with an ad or an offer for a free trial offer experience. At this point, they have "raised their hand," to get more information, so to speak.

Customer. A customer is someone who has purchased from you. A compelling offer to a prospect causes him or her to become a customer. But a customer who makes a purchase may or may not be loyal. Customers may or may not return or refer others to you.

Client. A client is someone who repeats a purchase, refers you, and relies on you to take care of his or her needs in that particular area. You transform customers into clients by delivering the most phenomenal service experience ever and staying in touch with them. For example, you may have your accountant, your attorney, your doctor, the person who takes care of your yard, your favorite airline, your favorite restaurant, and so on.

Phenomenal lifetime community member. This is a person who feels like he or she belongs to your community. You move people to this level by creating so many meaningful experiences over time that he or she almost feels part of your company. When I was building my first company, I had clients and referral sources who were so involved in my life, and mine in theirs, that we still feel like family today. Many times I was the only vendor invited to a client's company Christmas party. It's not unusual for our team to have openhearted encounters with clients who are having difficulties in their lives. Whether it is the loss of a child, relationship problems, or difficulties at work, they trust our team members to share with them.

My training and coaching company Phenomenal Products is ideally suited for building community because our clients are reaching for life goals and business success, which always leads them to examine every aspect of their lives. We are a community. Our coaching community volunteers and helps one another out. The result is radical life change ranging from saved marriages to debt elimination to impressive business growth. Our community has walked through cancer, deaths, and many other difficult situations with one another.

When you intentionally build community in your company and then intentionally create community experiences for your customers, clients, patients, members, donors, or guests, you'll make a meaningful contribution to their lives—and you'll also be poised to make bigger profits.

CONCLUSION: GIFT FROM THE SEA

Throughout this book, we've talked about the benefits of bigger profits and happier clients as a result of an inspired team, but that's not the biggest benefit of building community in your business and in your life.

Not by a long shot.

The gift from the SEA (support, encouragement, and accountability) is the most special gift of all: who you become as a leader and who your team members become. When you discover how to have an impact in another person's life, it's the most satisfying feeling in the world. As John Maxwell told me, "Once you get a taste of significance, success will never satisfy."

I agree with the subtitle of author Seth Godin's book *Tribes: We Need You To Lead Us*. There's a leadership vacuum in our world today. Especially leaders with positive values.

The time is now for business owners and managers to step up and become phenomenal leaders. The time is now to bring the special gift of community to a hurting world.

Every day the media delivers news of yet another shooting or terror attack. People need encouragement now. We all need the gift of the SEA to have the phenomenal life we all deserve.

We need one another.

We need community.

We need you.

The time is short.

The time is now.

Start the process by creating your first POD.

Download a free POD template for each of the chapters of this book at www.HowardPartridge.com/PODS.

INDEX

ABOUT THE AUTHOR

Howard Partridge is an international business coach with coaching members in over 100 industries in nine countries. He is a bestselling author of seven books, an executive vice president of Ziglar, Inc., and director of training operations. He is the founder and president of Phenomenal Products, Inc., which helps business owners and leaders improve their organizations by improving their leadership skills and systems, and is a Certified DISC Human Behavior Consultant.

Howard has been a business owner for more than 33 years and has been helping business owners and leaders for over two decades. He has helped small business owners around the world dramatically improve their businesses.

Howard grew up on welfare in Mobile, Alabama, and left home at 18. He arrived in Houston, Texas, on a Greyhound bus with only 25 cents in his pocket. Today, he leads world-class seminars that have included top business trainers such as John Maxwell, Michael Gerber, Bob Burg, Dr. Joseph A. Michelli, Darren Hardy, Dr. Robert Rohm, and Zig Ziglar.

Howard has been married to Denise for over 33 years and has one son named Christian who is 24.

Get free leadership and business growth resources at www.Howard Partridge.com.